MW01001999

# The
# Angels
# Have
# Left Us

Esther
Brown

*Hugh McCullum*

# The Angels Have Left Us

*The Rwanda Tragedy
and the Churches*

With a foreword by
Desmond Tutu

**Risk**
*BOOK SERIES*

**WCC Publications, Geneva**

Cover design: Edwin Hassink

Cover photo: Don Edkins

ISBN 2-8254-1154-X

© WCC Publications, World Council of Churches,
150 route de Ferney, 1211 Geneva 2, Switzerland
No. 66 in the Risk Book series

Printed in Switzerland

# Contents

For Kevin

# Foreword

When we come face to face with ghastly atrocities we are appalled and want to ask, "But what happened to these people that they should have acted in this manner? What happened to their humanity that they should have become inhumane?" Is that not how we felt when we encountered the horrors of the Holocaust or the dropping of the atomic bombs on Hiroshima and Nagasaki, when we heard of the horrible goings-on of an Idi Amin or a Bokassa, when we learned of the vicious occurrences in the killing fields of Cambodia and now the excesses in Bosnia and the genocide in Rwanda? We have been equally appalled by the gross violations of human rights in many Latin American countries.

Yes, we hang our heads in shame as we witness our extraordinary capacity to be vicious, cruel and almost devoid of humaneness. And yet that is surely not the only story that can be told of us human beings. We do have a noble side, which often amazes us — as when virtually the entire globe responds to disasters in one or another part of the world. Then it seems our generosity knows no bounds. We have experienced the remarkable capacity of people to forgive those who tortured, oppressed and abused them.

The story of Rwanda shows both these sides of our humanity. The churches were sometimes quite superb in what they did in the face of intimidation and at great cost to themselves. But there were other times when we failed dismally and seemed to be implicated in ways that have left many disillusioned, disgruntled and angry with the churches and their leadership. Many have been alienated and feel badly betrayed.

I hope that all of us will continue to pray for the broken and deeply traumatized people of Rwanda and that the church will be involved in a ministry of healing, of restoration, of forgiveness and reconciliation — not a cheap, but a costly reconciliation. I fear that if we concentrate too much on an international tribunal and its proper functioning to ensure that no one gets away with having committed gross violations of human rights and other atrocities, then those who will be brought to book and their ethnic groups will just wait for the chance to get their own back. Somehow the cycle of atrocity followed by reprisal and revenge followed by atrocity again will never be broken.

May we be blessed with the grace that will enable us to do what God wants us to do. Hugh McCullum has done us proud with the quality of his reporting out of Rwanda, reflected in this book, which should leave us all with deeply troubled consciences.

*Desmond Tutu*
*Anglican Archbishop of Cape Town, South Africa*
*President of the All Africa Conference of Churches*

# Acknowledgments

*My sacrifice is this broken spirit, you will not scorn this crushed and broken heart* (Psalm 51:17).

This book does not pretend to be the definitive analysis of the catastrophe that is Rwanda. I am a journalist, with all the failings and contradictions of that craft. I am not unfamiliar with the problems of covering complex and difficult war situations where nothing is quite as you think it is and few things are completely verifiable.

From April 7, 1994, until the end of the year, when this book was written, I produced thousands of words about Rwanda, a country I had visited only once before, in 1986, and about which I knew little except for vague notions of Hutu-Tutsi violence. Most of what I wrote was based on my own observations and interviews while travelling, often with other journalists, under dangerous and difficult circumstances.

The horror of Rwanda was like nothing I have ever before experienced, and it somehow for me broke through the studied detachment that is necessary for fair journalism. I found myself shocked, frightened, frustrated and, increasingly, enraged at the this thing called the international community and its almost obscene inability to understand, to act effectively and to speak consistently. A holocaust slipped by and *we didn't get it*, not because we didn't know but because, it seemed, we didn't care.

When we should have been acting with a sense of moral outrage, we became bureaucratic and rigid. When we should have been naming the evil as genocide, we calculated what the implications of such a statement might be on our partners and friends and economic communities. We competed expensively and extensively for scarce funds, outdoing one another in our efforts to promote our own agendas. The agenda of this so-called international community is unfettered humanitarianism, which has contributed greatly to Africa's current plight through ill-advised and questionable interference. Worse, it then turns its back when things get ugly and desperate.

I cannot help wondering cynically whether Rwanda's pain has been eased at all by this need to meddle and then, when that doesn't work, to blame it on weak, incompetent and

corrupt African leaders. What may have been eased is the
sense of guilt of the North and the financial crunch under
which some relief agencies found themselves labouring before
Rwanda exploded.

So this book is part cathartic and part critique. I hope it
may prod some to begin looking for better ways to act in
solidarity with Africa, rather than perpetuating a new colonial-
ism while Africa is still paying the price for the 19th-century
version.

Many people helped me. I must especially thank colleagues
at the All Africa Conference of Churches (AACC): general
secretary José Chipenda for his patience and support; André
Karamaga, Mutombo Mulami and Harold Miller for pointing
out all my misconceptions and helping me out of some of the
pitfalls lying in wait for the unsuspecting; my co-workers
Marcia Cruz, Mwendo Mutiso and Kambale Kavuo, who kept
the Information Desk going when no one knew where I was.

I want especially to acknowledge some Canadians who
made it possible to get in and out of Rwanda with a measure of
safety and certainty: Lucy Edwards, the Canadian high commissioner in Nairobi, who has Rwanda under her diplomatic
wing; the crews of the Canadian Forces Hercules, who dipsy-
doodled their way into Kigali almost every day past heat-
seeking missiles and ground-fire and about whose coolness and
competence I cannot say enough; Major Jean-Guy Plante for
helping me to get around and to learn that soldiers are human
too. My journalistic colleagues, despite all the unkind things I
have said about "the gospel according to CNN", were also
brave and good companions, especially Peter Maser of
Southam News Service and Jackie Nhorton of CBC, with
whom I often travelled. Thanks, too, to Jim Kirkwood of the
United Church of Canada, Rob Shropshire of the Anglican
Church of Canada and Gary Kenny of the Interchurch Coalition on Africa (ICCAF).

I have drawn extensively on reports by many organizations,
but especially *African Rights*, whose timely and in-depth publication *Rwanda: Death, Despair and Defiance* verified and
clarified my own observations. I have tried to acknowledge
wherever possible the use I made of their material. This, I trust,
will be a blanket statement of gratitude for their valuable work.

Thanks to Rebecca Garrett for taking on the task of editing on short notice and for making this book come out, I trust, in some readable fashion. I apologize for any factual errors or mistakes and accept full responsibility for whatever toes I may have stepped upon — deliberately or accidentally.

Finally, finally, as people say in Africa, I have been deeply and permanently awed by the courage and resilience of thousands of Rwandese men and women, the elderly and the young who stood heroically against death and for life.

# Rwanda
# From August 1994

Do you want to know what happened in Rwanda?

I have been there. I am there now.
Come, put your hand here on my chest and I will tell you.
Close your eyes. Listen.
Now push, push gently, gently.
Keep your eyes closed.
Push past my skin. Through my ribs. Let your hand move deep
    into my chest.
Touch my heart. Hold it. Feel it. Push through its cavities to the
    centre of my heart.

Now, listen closely. Open your eyes, slowly, and look deep into
    mine. There, can you see it? I have been lying here for some
    time. I do not know what happened to my family — it
    depends on who I am, on where I am.

I was a man, a woman, a child, a fetus. You know I was killed.

I was killed by the militia because I am a Tutsi.
I was killed by the army because I was Hutu and a member of an
    opposition party.
I was killed by my neighbours because I would not go with them
    to kill others.
I was killed because I sought to protect my neighbour's child.
I was killed by my priest because it was the price he had to pay
    to keep others alive.
I was killed by my wife, my husband, my children, my parents
    because they had to kill me or be killed.
They killed many like me, women, children, men who hap-
    pened to be here. I know why, but I don't know why.

I was killed by their machetes.
I was killed by their Kalishnakovs.
I was killed by their grenades.
I was killed by their bare hands.

I was killed by the rebels' soldiers when they arrived here.
They killed many like me, women, children, men who hap-
    pened to be here. I know why, but I don't know why.

I was killed by illness because we are so many, because we live so close, because there is so much sickness, because I am afraid to return home.

I was killed when I tried to leave the camps to go back and they did not want me to go.

I was killed when I returned home, by those I found on my land. Was it once their land?

I was killed when another said I had participated in the massacres. Did I? I was taken, arrested, and my family does not know where I am. They have asked, but no one will tell them. There was no trial — just an accusation.

I was killed in the war four years ago.

I was killed in massacres in my village two years back. I was killed earlier this year when someone threw a grenade into my house.

I was buried here by my family.

I was buried here in this mass grave and no one knows whether I am dead.

I died here in my grave after they forced me to dig it and put me and others inside it and shot us.

I have never been buried. I am in my house. I am in the woods. I was thrown in a river.

I have been left here as a testament to what happened, for you and for the world to see.

Do you understand now? No? Then keep you hand on my heart and look into yourself. Ask yourself what happened with Canadian troops in Somalia when a Somali teenager was tortured to death. Ask yourself if your parents or grandparents fought in our wars, if they prepared our troops to go overseas, if they killed. Why did they do this?

Now do you understand? No? Then look deeper. Ask yourself if you could kill. Ask yourself if you would kill if you thought it could save your family. If it would protect your neighbours. Your country. If it would protect your way of life against those you think would grab it away from you. If you believed that it would save what is important to you.

Ask yourself if you have ever looked at others as being
different from who you are yourself. You are Canadian.
Have you ever been angry at them for their differences?
Have you ever been angry at the French? At the English?
At Westerners? At Easterners? At Americans? At Muslims? At newcomers? At those born here? At people of
colour? At whites? When you hear about a murder here
now, do you wonder about the race of the killer? When
you are driving and someone cuts you off, do you look and
tell yourself, "They all drive like that?" Do you wonder
whether some people got jobs because they belong to a
particular group? Do you know of people who didn't get a
job because they are different?

If you answer "yes" to any of these questions, you will at least
understand how this began in my country. The inhumanity
we have known is human. It is in our human differences
that we have found reasons to dehumanize one another.
This is what I want to tell you. We have died, we have
killed because we are like you. I am like you. Now, I am
dead.

*Now has judgment come upon this world, now will this world's
prince be driven out, and I — once I am lifted up from the
earth — will draw all people unto myself* (John 12:31-32).

*It is the Lord who gives sight to the blind, who raises up those
who are bowed down, the Lord, who protects the stranger
and upholds the widow and orphan* (Psalm 146:8-9).

*Rob Shropshire*

---

Rob Shropshire is on the staff of the Africa/Middle East desk,
Primate's World Relief and Development Fund, Anglican Church of
Canada, Toronto. This poem was part of his trip report following a visit
to Rwanda and neighbouring countries from August 11 to September 6,
1994.

# Introduction

She is only 16, tall and slim, wearing a modest denim skirt and a dark blue cardigan wrapped over a faded print blouse. She holds herself painfully erect and stares ahead, eyes brooding and hooded. Shyly, she turns her back and pulls down the edge of the sweater from the smooth dark skin of her neck, revealing why she holds herself so sternly stiff. Three wide, ugly, corrugated-looking scars, still healing, slash their way across the velvet skin, cutting deep into muscle and nerves, leaving her permanently unable to turn her fine-boned head.

They did it with *pangas*, she says in a kind of husky whisper, referring to the all-purpose farm implement every Rwandese peasant carries like an extra limb. Her eyes, flat and expressionless, sweep across the verdant — but now unharvested — fields of sorghum. The nearby church compound stinks of death, and we step carefully to avoid the mounds of rotting corpses which are her relatives and friends, perhaps her brothers and sisters, maybe even her mother. Her father, she knows, was hacked to pieces somewhere nearby.

Her name is Josephine Uwamahoro, and she is a Tutsi who survived the charnel house that her Roman Catholic parish church had become at a hill called Ntarama. It doesn't appear on many maps of Rwanda, but it is not too far from the Burundi border in an area where many other Tutsis used to live.

Josephine took me and another Canadian journalist there one day in May 1994. A few days earlier I had joined with thousands of others to witness the glorious and enormously hopeful inauguration of Nelson Mandela as president of South Africa. There we saw sun on Africa's hauntingly beautiful horizon and said wisely to former comrades and friends that this was the dawn of a new era for this place called Africa, where man first stood upright and which much of the modern world has forsaken.

Josephine did not know about Mandela's stunning victory, or if she did it had little impact as we stood beside the red-brick church squatting forlorn in the scrub and long grass. Patches of brightly coloured material peeked out from the green landscape. It was a sort of pretty sight until the stench washed over us. As we drove up, our Ugandan driver Chamber pulled a handkerchief from his pocket and covered his nose. This gut-wrenchingly sweet smell of death hangs over every village in Rwanda like a pall of inescapable horror, and it will not go away even if the massacres have stopped — for a while anyway.

We were horrified but not surprised. This was not our first massacre-scene nor would it be the last. This was already my third trip into Rwanda since the killings began at almost precisely 8:30 p.m. on April 6. I would ultimately go a dozen times, many of them during heavy fighting. We set about our journalists' work carefully and silently, using our cameras as a kind of shield from the numbing bloodshed that had soaked the rich red earth of one of Africa's most fertile countries.

The bleached white skulls, still covered in tufts of curly black hair, stared up sightlessly into the camera lens. Many were split open like melons, mouths drawn tight with toothy grimaces. Claws of once-warm and caring hands were drawn close around tiny bodies mutilated and crushed by clubs and *pangas*.

The church doors were jammed half shut with corpses. The windows had been blown in by fragmentation grenades just to make certain that no one had escaped the slashing carnage. Inside was a slaughterhouse with bodies piled a metre deep under, beside and on top of the rough wooden benches. The whitewashed walls were splattered with gore, bloody palm-prints etched onto the rough walls in one last beseeching plea for mercy. A crucifix was snapped in two, its upstretched arms cut away from the rest of the symbol of the one whose sacrifice for all humanity was regularly celebrated on the altar of the euchar-ist. The small wooden altar itself was lying crazily askew with a decomposing body draped across one side.

"What do you call this?", my colleague asked. It is more than slaughter, more than insanity, more than desecration. There are no gas chambers in Rwanda, just bleeding churches and schools and hospitals.

Meanwhile Josephine and Chamber, who had never been to Rwanda before, are outside staring at these two very foreign journalists recording this trail of skeletons for voyeuristic audiences in a land which has never known war, many thousands of kilometres away.

Josephine's own story is told in the sibilant tones of the Kinyarwanda language shared by Hutus and Tutsis. It has been told dozens of times to a world that could not cope with this enormous evil and so turned its face away like the priest and the Levite of the parable of the Good Samaritan. Josephine had been saved because the raging, screaming mob of militias, none of whom she knew, had hacked her neck and legs early in the slaughter. Unconscious, she had fallen to the floor of the church where she had been baptized and received her first communion, her blood mingling with that of her neighbours. Their corpses fell on top of her wounded body, saving her from the madness. When the grenades were tossed into the building, the bodies of others saved her life.

Slipping in and out of awareness she heard the killers — *interahamwe* in her language — offering to "sell" a bullet to someone for 4000 Rwandese francs, perhaps ten US dollars. Shooting is less painful than a club or *panga* but more expensive. Josephine passed out and awoke, weak and frightened, long after it was over, under a pile of still warm bodies. It took her all night to crawl from her people's tomb to a school where she found some women from another hill. They cared for her and hid her, with their own children, in a slimy papyrus swamp for a month and she recovered, at least in her body.

She tells us the whole story in a flat unemotional voice, no tears, no paralyzing grief, just a harrowing story of losing all your family, all your loved ones, all your friends — everyone you have known during your entire 16 years. It is a story we heard too often in those thick dark days. Many of us have lost a close friend or a loved one and know the emotion-draining ache of that experience, but I cannot comprehend what Josephine is feeling. Is it grief, or trauma, or simply survival? I cannot get my Western mind around these questions and so my colleague and I go about our professional tasks. The pain of incomprehension comes later.

An international news magazine published a stark cover on May 16 quoting a missionary: "There are no devils left in Hell. They are all in Rwanda." The last thing I remember about Josephine is her standing in that strangely erect posture and whispering to us: "We will never come back to this church. It is a graveyard. The angels have left us."

Then we leave, and there is nothing to say for a very long time as our troubled minds try to grope through the thick darkness and gloom of what we have seen and heard. We creep into Kigali and another night of shelling, and sleep does not come for a long time in the room of a murdered priest in the stricken Christus Centre.

## Never again...

The Christus Centre is a Jesuit house for social and cultural studies, near Amahoro Stadium in a suburb of Kigali. In 1986 I had attended a meeting there with colleagues from Geneva. Amid the pleasant green surroundings, we had discussed communication theory and practice. In Room 28, eight years later, seventeen priests and nuns were machine-gunned to death on April 8. A small carved wooden crucifix still hangs amid the swirls and contortions of the bloody walls, the cement blocks pocked with AK-47 bullet holes. A tiny jar with dried flowers sits outside on the walkway where we had once earnestly debated the meaning of the information revolution for the ecumenical movement.

The bodies are buried now and some of the survivors are back. But the two hand-prints we saw etched in blood on the wall will be there always. So will memories of the desk calendar of the priest in whose room we tried to sleep, opened silently to April 8, his breviary with coloured ribbons marking the readings for that day, his pyjamas still hanging neatly on a hook. His body is now in a mass grave not far from Room 28.

It wasn't supposed to be this way after the delirious joy of South Africa. It is too much to comprehend. The world said in 1945 it would never happen again. Genocide is too daunting for our fragile, pampered psyches and too complex for our equally fragile and pampered international structures. So rather than confront the evil that is among us, we look away. Some of us write cheques to allow the new mercenaries, the international relief workers in their neatly pressed khakis, to assuage our guilt while our leaders debate the niceties of whether it was genocide or just a crime against humanity.

Jewish friends talk of their frustration that the world always forgets the Holocaust. In Kigali on those days when we were caught between two fighting armies and bands of militias in the dubious shelter of the Hotel Amaharo where the UN had its headquarters, we would talk about that Holocaust and remember our parents saying, "Never again." But the mute corpses lying in one last contorted embrace in a church compound cry out that it had happened again, and that it was done this time with the grisly intimacy of slashing machetes and nail-studded clubs.

The world "discovered" Rwanda in mid-May, coincidentally about the same time as CNN did, when refugees began pouring into Tanzania to Ngara, immediately dubbed the "largest refugee camp ever". But then came the flood of refugees into Goma, in Zaïre, and the spectacle of humanitarianism out of control. By that time, a million people, more or less, had been slaughtered in Rwanda, but the world took little notice and the United Nations ran away.

Ignoring or avoiding warnings that it was genocide, we instead became fixated on Goma and Ngara. But the story of Rwanda is not that of a cholera epidemic, terrible as it was. It is not the story of hundreds of thousands of refugees establishing camps in Tanzania which exactly replicated the conditions and systems in Rwanda that allowed killers to operate with impunity (and they are still there, terrorizing and brutalizing the squalid refugee camps of eastern Zaire and western Tanzania).

Cholera and other diseases, orphans and masses of desperate refugees are the consequence of the genocide. The international community and the worldwide church cannot wash away that central horror with humanitarian emergency aid which in itself became an obscenity. The incompetence and inadequacy of the relief effort in May and July were bad enough. More appalling was the proliferation of 149 international agencies, including many churches, blanketing Kigali with a suffocating screen of speeding white vehicles and flags and stickers and briefings. Many failing aid agencies who would not have been able to find Rwanda on a map six months earlier were "saved" by the refugees in Goma and Ngara.

But the central horror — the one we want to go away, the one the United Nations and the United States could not deal with — was the genocide. Why did it happen when everyone in Rwanda — churches, UN representatives, the Organization of African Unity (OAU), non-governmental organizations (NGOs), politicians — knew months before that something terrible had been planned and organized and was ready to go? Why could it not have been stopped? Why did the UN pull out? What can be done to prevent it from happening again in

Rwanda? In Burundi? In Nigeria? In Afghanistan? In Bosnia? In Russia? Wherever?

The world knew of the Holocaust in Nazi Germany and did nothing until it was too late; the world knew what was happening in Rwanda and did nothing until it was too late. Have our human instincts become so blunted and numbed that we can act only when it is too late? My friend and colleague and boss at the AACC delivered himself of an uncharacteristic outburst one day late in 1994 in Kigali when he told expatriate staff of Church World Action-Rwanda (CWA-R) that the church had sent missionaries to Africa during the colonial period. "Now," said José Chipenda, "you are sending us *mercenaries*."

It is a sign of the depths of our powerlessness and cynicism that we now look for "explanations" for the Rwanda holocaust in over-population, land pressures, ecological degradation, the colonial legacy, French manipulation, debt, "globalization", the collapse of the nation state, moral vacuums, political venality, ethnic extremism…, and the list becomes endless. All are more or less factors, to be sure, but genocide, the gravest, most notorious crime against humanity recognized by international law, goes unpunished for lack of international will and the North's need to rationalize its inaction in the face of the deliberate, organized and efficient deaths of a million people.

Genocide, planned meticulously, executed with extraordinary cruelty and implicating almost every surviving Hutu in one way or another was what happened in Rwanda. Until that is named and owned by the international community, moral confidence cannot return to Rwandese whether they are Hutu or Tutsi, whether they are stranded in festering refugee camps or trying to expropriate someone else's house in Kigali.

If all the West has to offer is a kind of "reluctant humanitarianism" (*African Rights Report*), there will surely be more genocides in Rwanda. I remember well a meeting one July day in Nairobi when the AACC was trying to bring some sense to it all. A crusty old Africa hand working for the International Committee of the Red Cross was there. The ICRC was one of only two international agencies which operated in Rwanda during the 100-day war; the other 147 came after July 4 when the war ended. He had been in one emergency or another for the last 25 years, and he came close to tears when he said, "We cannot cope with one more disaster here in Africa." A day or two later, we were on the same plane to the new disaster site of Goma.

## Beyond humanitarianism

We have somehow to get beyond humanitarianism. Raising many millions of dollars because decent, caring members of congregations in the North want us "to do something" for Rwanda and know of no other way to deal with the pictures except to send money is a way to assuage our domestic constituency. Sending little boxes of goodies to orphans at Christmas time, as an outfit called Samaritan's Purse did (accompanied by paid photographers and journalists), may make us feel a bit better, although somehow it seems hollow when the killers of their parents are living with impunity and fomenting trouble in the refugee camps. The former head of Médecins sans Frontières (MSF) calls this the "morality of the ambulance".

The massacres are over, the gruesome pictures have faded from our television screens and we organize for the next emergency, perhaps in Rwanda again or in Burundi. There is precious little talk of justice, but then there never has been in such situations. The notion of development — real development, not the kind practised by the lords of poverty and the merchants of misery — has been consigned to the rubbish heap of history. There is far more attention and glory to be earned by parachuting pallets of food on the heads of refugees in time for the evening TV news spots than by supporting notions of civil society and human rights and more classrooms and dispensaries.

To deal with Africa through the medium of horror stories and ill-conceived humanitarianism is to ignore the oppressive economic system benignly known as globalization, to avoid the all-pervasive cultural imperialism of the US and European communications industry, to keep silent about the delivery of expensive weapons from Egypt (paid for by France) and from the burgeoning arms industry in newly beloved South Africa.

There is a serious danger that this turning away from reality will further marginalize an increasingly marginalized continent, writing off the resilience and resources and talents and hopes and future of 650 million of God's people. Worse is the danger of recolonizing Africa in the name of stopping the descent into chaos. With economies controlled through the World Bank, the democratic process in the hands of the ubiquitous tourists known as "election monitors", good governance "assured via Western multi-partyism", security taken over by UN mercenaries, social services in the hands of the even more ubiquitous NGOs and resource development controlled by transnationals, what is left for an African government to do other than put its sticky fingers into the nearly empty cookie jar? And even corruption is underdeveloped in Africa, if you compare it with the savings and loans scandals in the US, for example.

The chaos the North wishes to prevent comes all too close to home as we watch the spectacle of politicians in the North making the poor and immigrants and people of colour the victims of their own attempts to cope with global free markets.

For the church, the fundamental, unwavering biblical imperative is that of justice. In the name of justice the church should talk of peace and reconciliation, knowing full well that justice comes first in that process. Instead, in the name of justice, it engages in short-term humanitarianism.

Justice is the only way Rwanda can be healed and the suppurating sore of hatred lanced so that the tiny traumatized country can be reconciled and reconstructed. Justice means naming the genocide, recognizing the root causes of the madness, punishing the perpetrators and, perhaps above all, supporting Rwandese in their overwhelming grief. Trying to short-circuit this process by concentrating on guilt-motivated humanitarianism is to fulfil the worst fears of one of my more jaded journalistic colleagues, who told me that he just wanted to go home to Zimbabwe and hug his kids... "but I'm afraid before long, Hugh, we'll be back."

# 1. The Tangled Tale of History

The popular but dangerously simplistic wisdom about Rwanda's catastrophe is that it was a primitive, savage eruption of ethnic (or tribal) rivalry, taking its place alongside Africa's other convulsions of mindless violence. Apart from the thinly veiled racism of this analysis, which too easily ignores the growing violence today in Europe or in the cities of the US or on the Aboriginal reserves of Canada and the bloody warfare of Desert Storm or the Occupied Territories or East Timor, it allows the international community to shrug off its complicity.

Rwandese Prime Minister Faustin Twagiramungu, a Hutu who steadfastly opposed the vicious machinations of the extremists, fiercely disputes the ethnic explanation of the violence.

I interviewed him in the smelly, bedraggled fifth-floor suite of rooms he was using as an office and living quarters in the once-luxurious Meridien hotel. Here, where journalists were holed up during the deadly war as the two armies lobbed mortars and grenades over our heads and sometimes into the walls and windows, the prime minister's laundry was now flapping on the balcony. While ethnicity played an important role in the genocide, he said, it was much more than traditional Hutu-Tutsi rivalry.

> It is ridiculous. We could be among the luckiest people in Africa. We have the same language, the same religions. There is no song or dance or drum-beat that is peculiar to one or the other of our people. We had disputes before the colonial period over things like land-ownership, and sometimes there were little fights, but the chiefs dealt with it in the traditional way and never did we suffer destruction like we have just experienced.

And, say the Catholic bishops of the region, there is nowhere else in Africa except neighbouring Burundi, also embroiled in similar paroxysms of violence, where you can find such commonality. "There are 13 million people in this sub-region who have everything in common, including almost total Christianity, and a long history, so we must look elsewhere for answers — and solutions — to this genocide," said seven bishops from the Roman Catholic Association of Member Episcopal Conferences of East Africa (AMECEA) in a thoughtful analysis after visiting Rwanda.

History supports the contention that the violence in Rwanda was about power — about wanting so much to keep absolute power as to justify any evil.

## Historical uncertainty and racist myths

Rwanda is so small it would fit into Ireland with plenty of room left over, but about eight million people are crammed into its 25,000 square kilometres, making it the most densely populated country in Africa and one of the most densely populated in the world.

Most historians agree that Rwanda and Burundi were probably occupied originally by Twa hunter-gatherers, now less than one percent of the population, who for centuries were erroneously and offensively categorized as "pygmies" and relegated to the margins of society. Later, farming Hutus and cattle-herding Tutsis migrated to this fertile area, well-watered by the many lakes and rivers that cut into its valleys and hills.

There is some dispute about who arrived first, but the popular notion that the Tutsis, coming from Ethiopia, invaded Rwanda and established a kingdom over the Hutus is now refuted by students of the region. The two are not different ethnic groups; rather, they are social categories, because neither established a language, culture or territory of its own. The minority Tutsi (14 percent of population), who arrived last in what is now Rwanda, were mainly pastoralists, and the Hutu majority (85 percent) mainly farmers.

The racist theories of the early colonizers in the 18th century persuaded them that physical appearances — Tutsis tall and slim with straight noses and long fingers ("more like us"), Hutus more "Bantu" in appearance, shorter with broad noses and stubby fingers — were an indicator of intelligence and ability. Missionaries and colonizers even developed a now-debunked theory that Tutsis were Hamitic people who may have been Christianized in Ethiopia, making them more open to re-evangelization and genetically and intellectually superior to Hutus. First the German, then the Belgian colonizers developed this theory, delegating power and privilege to the minority Tutsi in classic divide-and-rule colonial tactics. Sadly, many Rwandese accepted this racist theory, even though they themselves will say that physical characteristics are misleading in identifying one group or the other. That has led to the ethnic rivalries of the 20th century.

From about the 17th century rival clans developed along strict hierarchical lines divided between farmers, herders and warriors who became chiefs and, in some cases, monarchs. Wars over land and cattle-stealing occasionally broke out but were traditionally dealt with through some form of negotiation. As time went by certain religious practices — drumming, sacred fire and ceremonies around crops and cattle — emerged, which led to god-like kings of Hutus and Tutsis.

Gradually one kingdom became stronger than the other small kingdoms and held a kind of political and administrative dominance. Called the Nyiginya, these Tutsis tended to exploit the Hutu farmers through an elite caste system and slowly gained power over what is now Rwanda. But recent historians point out that the monarchy contained elements of both earlier Hutu and Tutsi clans or monarchies. Intermarriage occurred, and as the Nyiginya consolidated their power, a clan system covered the country which for some generations was more pervasive than the Hutu-Tutsi-Twa designations. Cattle was the dominant form of wealth, also giving the Tutsis greater power.

By the turn of the century, the Rwandese were ruled by a single monarch. In a well-organized and stratified culture, power was held by Tutsi kings and chiefs but there were also clearly identifiable Hutu areas. The ethnic divide was in reality more of a political divide, although based on ancestry.

When the Germans colonized the country, they immediately identified the royal Tutsis as their favourites and exploited the pre-colonial structures. With Belgian trusteeship under the League of Nations after the first world war, the racialization of the political reality was exploited, and the position of the Tutsis as the ruling elite was gradually institutionalized by giving them educational advantages and administrative positions.

Hutus were systematically excluded from all levels of power and left in a subordinate position. After the conversion of the king to Christianity in 1931, even the Roman Catholic Church identified with the Tutsi leadership. Hutus were often pressed into forced labour, a kind of slavery that was legally abolished only in 1927.

From this time until independence fever swept Africa in the early 1960s, the seeds of distrust and animosity sown by colonial favouritism and exploitation grew. Small cliques of Tutsis held power, but the majority of Tutsis were as poor as the Hutus. Later, a small clique of Hutus became powerful extremists, but the majority of Hutus remained poor and outside the realms of power.

From the beginning the Catholic Church enjoyed a cosy relationship with the Belgian colonizers and the Tutsi royal court, quickly becoming the second most powerful institution in the country. A few small Protestant missions of the Reformed and Anglican traditions were established late in the 19th century by missionaries from Belgium, Britain, Denmark and Switzerland.

Not only was the church in those colonial times divided along Tutsi-Hutu lines, but, worse, it propagated the notion of ethnic superiority. By controlling all educational facilities in Rwanda, the church ensured that some Tutsis at least had enough education to become administrators and to consolidate power and gain wealth.

The Roman Catholics became a *de facto* state church. Although Hutus were converted, it was not until the 1950s that the church switched its allegiance from the Tutsi ruling class to the Hutu majority (leaving them open to new accusations of ethnic favouritism). By independence in 1961 the Catholic Church was overly connected with the dominant Hutu republics. Protestants were less tainted with overt ethnicity, though some denominations were quietly known as Hutu- or Tutsi-dominated.

At the root of today's tragedy, it would seem, is mutual fear and loathing — the Tutsis afraid of individual and collective extermination, the Hutus of further subjection and exploitation. Some of this fear is rooted in history and clearly in the colonial tactics of divide-and-rule so common in Africa.

The Hutus began agitating for power in the late 1950s with the publication of a manifesto by Parmehutu (Party for the Emancipation of the Hutu People), reacting to the exclusive rule exercised by the Tutsi clan leaders. The manifesto was drawn up by Gregoire Kayibanda, who would become president of Rwanda's First Republic. He had been personal secretary to the

Roman Catholic Archbishop André Perraudin and editor of a Catholic newspaper.

The Belgians, always quick to abandon their clients when rebellions broke out, dumped the Tutsi leadership and, allegations have it, had the king killed by a lethal injection during a visit to Burundi. At any rate, a violent uprising began in the north of the country, ultimately killing as many as 15,000 Tutsis while thousands more fled to neighbouring Uganda, Zaire, Tanzania and Burundi, where they later formed the nucleus of the Rwandan Patriotic Front (RPF).

## Post-independence tensions

Although Parmehutu did not start this first round of massacres, it benefitted from it to strengthen the racial ideology of Hutu power. On July 1, 1962, supported by Belgian paratroopers, Kayibanda became president of the First Republic, launching what he called a social revolution and proclaiming Rwanda the country of the Bahutus. The Parmehutu aim was to promote Hutu clan solidarity against what it called Tutsi feudalism. In essence, this simply exchanged one set of dominant structures for another, but it was enough for the oppressed and desperately poor peasants — at least for a few months.

Identity cards were retained. These had been introduced by the Belgians in the 1930s and identified each person as Hutu, Tutsi or Twa, a designation which could not be changed except by paying an enormous bribe. Old and discredited racial theories once used by Tutsis against Hutus were now used against the former rulers.

Exiled Tutsis — called *inyenzis* or cockroaches — fought back from outside but were easily defeated by the Belgian-trained army, which could and did call in the paratroopers to save Kayibanda's presidency. The result however was to create enormous tensions among the Hutu peasants, resulting in reprisal massacres in 1963, which killed 20,000 people and sent 100,000 as refugees to Burundi. Throughout the 1960s a series of massacres left the country in a state of fear and violence orchestrated by the increasingly powerful army, destabilizing Parmehutu's southern-based party and dramatically weakening Kayibanda's authority.

6

Although Parmehutu succeeded in purging Tutsis from most positions of authority and educational opportunities — except in the Catholic Church — the government was corrupt and discredited. Another wave of ethnic assaults on Tutsis in 1973 resulted in a military coup led by Major General Juvenal Habyarimana, a northerner who announced a moral revolution and an end to ethnic politics. Development and balance were the general's mottos, and for a few months people believed that the virulent antagonisms could be set aside.

In 1975, Habyarimana launched the Second Republic with a new constitution which called for a single party, the *Mouvement révolutionnaire pour le développement et la démocratie* (MRND), the National Revolutionary Movement for Development and Democracy.

Despite Habyarimana's lofty aims of balance and development, his regime quickly became autocratic and corrupt, switching privileges from the south to the north, to the area around Gisenyi, which was the town nearest Habyarimana's *colline*, the hill where he was born, creating a second power struggle. Tutsis were excluded from key positions, and southerners were regarded as too "infected" by the Tutsis to be trusted in a truly Hutu nation. The *African Rights* report points out that the majority of Hutu politicians targeted for execution after Habyarimana's death were from the south.

It is important also to see the all-pervasive concentration of power by Habyarimana from 1973 until 1990 as he and his coterie dispensed privileges to northern relatives and friends at the expense of the rest of the country. For about a decade, the Tutsi problem was thought to have been solved through massacres, refugee exoduses and marginalization. Only in Uganda, which Habyarimana seems strangely to have ignored, did hopes for Tutsi resurgence keep burning.

Poverty and over-population, land pressures and ecological degradation have all been advanced as reasons for Rwanda's tensions, and undoubtedly they were factors in the constant unrest in Rwanda. But none of them explains genocide.

It is true that Rwanda had one of the highest female fertility rates in the world. The population increased from 2.8 million at independence to more than 7.5 million in 1990, with a density of 285 people per square kilometre. It is also true that land is scarce: 57 percent of farmers own less than a hectare. When Tutsis fled, their lands were usually occupied by Hutus, who then feared that a return of the *inyenzi* would cost them what little they had. Habyarimana exploited the demographic data for his own ends, arguing that refugees could not return because of land scarcity. The proponents of the over-population explanation also ignore Rwanda's incredibly rich soil and good rainfall.

Rwanda earned about 75 percent of its foreign exchange from the export of coffee and a small amount from tourism in the famous Volcanoes National Park, where the rare mountain gorillas attracted thousands of visitors each year. Both these foreign currency generators were subject to market forces and instability. By the 1980s the economy was in a state of decay despite the US$200 million a year received from overseas donors who liked the easy administrative structure and clear lines of responsibility, leaving the strong-arm government rife with corruption and favouritism. Aid was concentrated in the north, and ministers and prefects routinely siphoned off their cut. Habyarimana's friends and relatives, especially those of his wife Agathe (now living in comfortable exile in Nairobi), built huge fortunes from the aid business. They were known as *Akazu* and were extremely jealous of their privileges, which the extremists among them were prepared to defend even to genocide.

The growing military — up from 5000 in 1990 to 35,000 in 1993 — and bureaucracy gave MRND the patronage system it needed to control its poverty-stricken populace. Rwanda has a local government system of 10 prefectures divided into 143 communes administered by burgomeisters (mayors). These are further divided into sectors run by elected councillors, who in turn have a total of 8500 cells, directed by chiefs. Many of these functionaries and their administrative support are government appointees.

Like all African cities, Kigali was teeming with thousands of unemployed young people living off crime, prostitution and the informal economy. For those privileged with education and power, it was a pleasant enough place, with large villas and modern buildings strung out along its many hills. The infrastructure was good, telecommunications excellent, office buildings modern and hospitals and schools well-run. For the wealthy and expatriates it was a fun sort of place with an overlay of

French *joie de vivre*. For many, though, it was a place of poverty and terror. Structural adjustment programmes imposed by international financial institutions intensified the impoverishment of the majority poor rural and urban populations, making them easy recruits for political and ethnic extremists and for filling the ranks of the militias for a few extra francs.

Tutsis were excluded from almost all aspects of civil society and were forced by this discrimination into commerce or the professions because of their higher degree of education dating from the colonial period.

While all these factors made Rwanda a tempestuous and strife-filled little country, they do not explain genocide. Many other countries in Africa and elsewhere in the world have similar or worse problems. They have constant droughts, real tribalism, some even civil wars. They have poor land, dreadful degradation of the environment, corruption and favouritism. But they do not have genocide.

**Return from exile**

The RPF was formed out of the remnants of Yoweri Museveni's National Resistance Army in Uganda, which overthrew Tito Okello after the latter had overthrown the Milton Obote regime in 1986 and formed a government which is now the darling of the international investment community. Many of the NRA commanders were Tutsis from Rwanda who had been in exile since 1959. Numbering some 200,000, the Tutsis had become English-speaking and were integrated into Ugandan society.

After 1986, some of the NRA commanders, including Paul Kagame, now Rwanda's vice-president and minister of defence, secretly created the RPF, only later seeking Museveni's support. Well-armed, well-trained, well-disciplined and with years of bush-fighting experience, some 1500 rebels invaded Rwanda on October 1, 1990, with the express purpose of fighting their way into some kind of power-sharing with Habyarimana.

The Rwandese Armed Forces (FAR), though trained by French professional soldiers, well-equipped and much larger than the RPF, were poorly motivated. Habyarimana, always close to Zairean President Mobutu Sese Sekou, asked for help from him and from the French, who played a decisive role in preventing RPF from scoring a major victory. The fighting was fierce but neither side could win, and by the end of March 1991 a ceasefire was negotiated which included a neutral monitoring group and political talks with the MRND.

The next three years were marked by mutual mistrust, outright lies and a distinct lack of movement towards democracy despite promises in writing that multi-partyism would be introduced. Several new parties were formed, most of them led by Hutu moderates fed up with Habyarimana's corruption and oppression. The parties spanned the spectrum from Christian Democrats through Social Democrats but the most dangerous to the MRND was the MDR (Democratic Republican Movement), which claimed the old and tattered Parmehutu mantle and drew its support from the south and centre of the country. None of the four new parties had any ties to the RPF.

Habyarimana resorted to the long-standing practice in Rwanda of division by infiltrating the opposition and splitting its goal of peaceful change. The result was three years of political paralysis and confrontation. Violence was constant and with impunity. The extremist wing of the MRND, largely from the north, was known as the CDR (Coalition for the Defence of the Republic). It began organizing and arming militias and the notorious *interahamwe* ("those who stand together"). When it suited him, Habyarimana was always able to dissociate himself from the CDR, claiming they were a separate movement over which he exercised no control.

Several protocols were signed and a coalition government formed with a 19-member cabinet (10 of whom were from the ruling party), which was supposed to organize multi-party national elections within a year. But Habyarimana was not serious and quickly dismissed his first prime minister, a member of the MDR.

Human rights violations grew in intensity during this period. An international commission declared publicly that 2000 dissidents had been killed under direct orders of MRND officials, including the president, but no action was taken except to persecute political dissidents even more harshly.

Hundreds of people have spoken out about this period and the consequent breakdown of the most minimal forms of justice. Amnesty was awarded to the worst killers.

"In Rwanda all kinds of corruption, murder, torture, summary arrests and disappearances occurred from 1991-93 with impunity," says Jean Nepomucene Nayinzira, Hutu Christian Democratic Party (PCD) leader and a proposed cabinet minister in the transitional government. As we huddled beside a ragged tent in a displaced persons camp near Byumba where he had fled, he told me:

> It was this notion of impunity that rotted our society. The *Akazu* were involved up to their ears in drug rackets, prostitution, extortion, bribery and murder. They were allowed to function with impunity. No wonder they were nervous about power-sharing. We might have asked some direct questions. This idea of impunity must be purged from Rwanda society and throughout Africa if we are ever to have peace and some measure of prosperity.

Nayinzira said many of the political assassinations were ordered by Habyarimana himself and carried out by his elite French-trained Presidential Guard.

The turmoil continued until neighbouring countries, notably Tanzania, and the OAU began a round of negotiations with support from the UN, Belgium and Germany at the tourist town of Arusha, Tanzania. On August 5, 1993, five protocols were signed which brought the RPF into the equation after it had broken a ceasefire in February by trying to attack Kigali (an attack that might have succeeded — and prevented the horrors that were to follow a year or so later — except for the intervention of French troops on the side of the FAR).

The protocols covered respect for human rights and the rule of law, power-sharing, a transitional government, reform of all institutions of government, including the military and presidency, repatriation and resettlement of refugees, integration of RPF and FAR forces into a new, smaller army and demobilization of the Presidential Guard.

The RPF was allowed to have a 600-member battalion stationed in Kigali to protect RPF members of the transitional cabinet and national assembly while the United Nations Assistance Mission for Rwanda (UNAMIR) was set up to monitor the implementation of the accords. The transitional institutions were to have been in place within 37 days, when Faustin Twagiramungu of the MDR was to become prime minister.

Until then, the existing power-sharing arrangements continued with Agathe Uwilingiyimana, also of MDR, as interim prime minister. Both were Hutus.

## The failure of Arusha

From the beginning everything began to go horribly wrong. The clique of northerners around Habyarimana, the *Akazu*, aware that their power and privilege were close to an end and that they might have to face justice without impunity, deployed every tactic available to derail the accords. In this they had plenty of unwitting help from the international community.

The opposition, infiltrated by extremists fanatically loyal to the MRND and members of the CDR wing, quickly fell to squabbling among themselves. This was especially true of the MDR, which was the greatest threat to MRND hegemony because of its strength among Hutus in the central and southern regions of the country. Other parties also became factionalized to the point that they could not agree on positions in the transitional government and Habyarimana had all the excuses he needed to postpone implementation of the Arusha Accords.

It took the UN five months to get its forces in place to oversee the transition, and the World Bank blocked all funds to Rwanda until there was a government with which it could negotiate, further destabilizing the country and fanning the flames of hatred. By the time the RPF troops arrived at their base in the handsome National Development Council buildings in Kigali (the former National Assembly), the country was in a state of constant crisis. Political assassinations were routine and brutal, massacres were common and often unreported, political parties were mutating and militias of CDR extremists were setting up roadblocks even in downtown Kigali.

Nayinzira, frail and clearly distraught by the ordeal which almost cost him his life, told me in Byumba that by the end of 1993 Habyarimana was

> using all his powers to eliminate us physically and to buy off anyone he could in an effort to postpone forever the accords he had signed. He had several colleagues in other parties killed, which he then blamed on the RPF. His only purpose was to destabilize the country so as to avoid implementing the Arusha Accords at all costs. I think he was under extreme pressure from the *Akazu*,

especially from his wife, whose family had grown extremely rich and owned the fascist radio station which was to play a major role in fomenting hatred.

Habyarimana, now in his role as Transitional President, repeatedly postponed the swearing-in ceremonies of Uwilingiyimana's cabinet while at the same time arming and training more militias with help from the French. UNAMIR seemed impotent and by March 15 was threatening to withdraw if some progress was not made within a few weeks. The special representative of the UN secretary general, Cameroonian diplomat Jacques Roger Booh Booh, notable primarily for his willingness to compromise with Habyarimana, was fed up and recommended withdrawal of UNAMIR's 2500 soldiers. Despite the stalemate, the Security Council renewed UNAMIR's limited mandate to monitor the ceasefire and assist in ensuring the security of Kigali on April 5, the day before a regional summit to discuss the Rwanda crisis was to be held in Dar es Salaam.

Meeting in the Hotel Kilimanjaro, the heads of state of Uganda, Kenya and Burundi and the secretary general of the OAU, hosted by Tanzanian President Ali Hassan Mwinyi, brought enormous pressure on Habyarimana, who is reported to have given in and promised immediate implementation of the accords. Then he returned to Kigali in his Mystère Falcon executive jet, a gift from the French government that reflected the close personal relationship between the family of President François Mitterand and the Habyarimanas. He was accompanied by Burundi's newly appointed president Cyprien Ntaryamira, who changed his plans at the last minute and decided to accompany Habyarimana to Kigali, from where the French crew would take him on to Bujumbura.

At 8:30 p.m. on April 6, 1994, the sleek presidential jet was blasted out of the sky by three hand-held heat-seeking missiles. Ironically, chunks of the plane and bodies of its passengers plummeted into the gardens of the posh presidential mansion on the outskirts of Kigali and adjacent garages filled with expensive cars.

\* \* \*

Juvenal Habyarimana had become at 57 the ultimate victim of his own extremist ideology. The signal to begin the genocide had been given. Within 100 days a million people would die and half Rwanda's population would become displaced.

At this point, the international community turned away, leaving a few lone voices to raise questions about the human consequences of suffering and death, the political consequences of ongoing regional instability, the criminal consequences else-where of genocide and the moral consequences of a lack of compassion and responsibility.

# 2. The Making of Genocide: International Responsibility

Rwanda was no frantic explosion of bloodlust, sparked by the anger of a people whose beloved president was shot out of the sky. Rather, it was a careful and long-prepared plan to destroy a people. Press reports at the end of 1994 were still talking about a country losing its sanity, but that is too simplistic an analysis. What happened in Rwanda was premeditated murder, a genocide with clear motives, means and opportunity to carry it out. The plane crash was merely the signal.

## A flourishing arms trade

Already before 1990 the Rwandese military began stockpiling expensive light and heavy weapons purchased discreetly from Egypt and South Africa and paid for, equally discreetly, by the French, ever concerned to maintain their influence in francophone Africa. Zaire, always ready to be beholden to France (where President Mobutu owns houses and banks keep much of his considerable wealth), was the main conduit for arms supplies through the end of the civil war in July 1994.

France is alleged to have supplied the ground-to-air missiles (*African Rights*) that brought down Habyarimana's aircraft, although who actually fired them is still the subject of considerable speculation. However, most Rwandese believe the triggers were pulled either by French marksmen or three members of the Presidential Guard, despite strenuous accusations by Habyarimana's successors that the RPF was solely responsible. The extremists went on to form an interim government two days later.

Egypt's foreign policy relationship with France, though somewhat murky, is usually co-operative. According to reports by arms experts (*Human Rights Watch Arms Project*), the US$6 million paid for arms by France was based on credit extended by the nationalized French bank Credit Lyonnais, to be redeemed in tea from the Mulindi plantation in Rwanda (once the RPF field headquarters) after the extremists had exterminated all opposition.

An angry senior RPF official told me emphatically that this transfer of money to purchase mortars, grenades, land mines, artillery and assault rifles made the genocide possible, whereas the thuggish government could previously manage only an occasional massacre. He also insisted that the withdrawal of UN forces after April 6 was due to close ties forged over many years with France by UN Secretary-General Boutros Boutros-Ghali, a former Egyptian foreign minister.

South Africa had no special relationship with either France or Rwanda, but its state-owned arms manufacturer Armscor saw a chance for profit in the sale of some 20,000 deadly fragmentation grenades, which were used by the militias to finish off many of the people seeking safety in churches during the killing days, as well as 10,000 rifle grenades, five thousand R4 automatic rifles and more than a million rounds of ammunition, worth US$5.9 million. All this was used to fight the civil war and to protect the less high-tech *interahamwe*. Along with the planting of hundreds of thousands of South African-made land mines in Angola, the deadly sales to Rwanda have sparked a serious campaign, led by South African churchmen like Anglican Archbishop Desmond Tutu and Methodist Bishop Peter Storey, to curb Armscor's activities and convert the technology to peaceful purposes. Given the profitability of Armscor at a time when South Africa needs all the foreign exchange it can get to rebuild the apartheid-shattered economy, the moral campaign is often thwarted by pragmatic politicians in the name of investment.

Some Rwandese officers were also trained in military schools in the US. As late as 1992, the Bush administration certified that "there is no evidence of any systematic human rights abuses by the military or by any other element of the government of Rwanda".

## Genocide: orchestrated and intimate

The victims of the genocide — surely unprecedented anywhere in the world for the sheer concentration of bloodshed and the brutality of the methods used — were neither blown away by nuclear weapons or "smart" bombs nor machine-gunned on a battlefield nor even shuttled by freight cars to gas chambers. They were killed up close by simple machetes (*pangas*) apparently imported in a large scale from China in 1993, and nail-studded clubs called *masus*. The intimacy of such killings, often carried out by relatives and neighbours, is far more chilling even than the efficiency of the Nazi killing machine.

France helped to train the Presidential Guard, the regular army, the gendarmerie (police) and the professional *interahamwe* (militias). French military advisors were specifically attached to the 1500-member (officially 600) Presidential Guard, most of whom came from Habyarimana's *colline*. The FAR was logistically well-equipped to support the massacres. The police, at all levels, especially at the commune level, were highly politicized and under the control of the local officials who owed their positions to the late president.

The *interahamwe* constituted a kind of civilian paramilitary force under the control of the MRND, established sometime in 1991 ostensibly to fight off the RPF invasion of Rwanda. They were, along with the Presidential Guard, the principal killers. These 1700 militia men and women were Hutu hardliners owned by the CDR, the extremist wing of the ruling party, and were highly trained in the art of killing. They were given uniforms and training at the Kanombe Barracks near Kigali airport by the French-trained Guardsmen. They were armed by the Ministry of Defence, although their allegiance was solely to the extremist politicians of the MRND and CDR, who paid young unemployed men salaries they could never hope to earn by legitimate means. They also had in effect a licence to loot — a phenomenon whose extent astounded journalists. Houses would be stripped first of valuables, then the remaining contents were taken — toilets, windows, door frames — until nothing was left. I recall seeing a young man trotting through the empty streets of Kigali carrying a bathtub on his shoulders and window frames through his arms, a big grin on his face.

The professional *interahamwe* rehearsed their gruesome trade in the two years leading up to the genocide by setting up random roadblocks to harass Tutsis, disrupting political meetings, terrorizing participants in peaceful anti-government demonstrations and generally orchestrating waves of violence and crime which some Rwandese observers have likened to the Nazi attacks on Jews, Gypsies and homosexuals in Germany before the second world war.

Rwandese fascists and their chiefs have decided to apply "the final solution" to their fellow citizens judged enemies of the regime. This refers to their political adversaries and defenceless populations. The existence of this criminal plan is no longer in doubt when we know it has just been denounced by Minister Félicien Gatabazi on Dec. 12, 1993 and by senior officers in a letter addressed to [UNAMIR Commander] General [Romeo] Dallaire, in which they denounce "the criminal designs of Habyarimana.

According to this article from the December 17, 1993, issue of *Journal Le Flambeau* and quoted in *African Rights*, there were 8000 non-professional *interahamwe* sufficiently trained and equipped who were waiting for the signal to begin assassinations among the residents of Kigali and its surroundings.

Some human rights organizations make a distinction between the professional killers and the ordinary people who joined the *interahamwe* and were trained and given arms after April 6. Most of the latter used low-technology weapons like *pangas* and *mazus* which, witnesses say, suddenly emerged from hidden storage places, unearthed as soon as radio reports signalled the death of Habyarimana.

However, it was not only the arming and training of killers that created the conditions for genocide. There was also the use of modern methods of propaganda during the last four years, frighteningly reminiscent of the extremely successful "big lie" philosophy of Josef Goebbels in the 1930s and 1940s.

A campaign of incitement to ethnic hatred was orchestrated and carried out by mass media owned and operated by members of Agathe Habyarimana's family and the government. Radio Rwanda was government-controlled. The notorious Radio Television Mille Collines (RTLM), established privately only in 1993, played a central role in encouraging genocide by whipping up fratricidal fears of a return to Tutsi massacres and domination among illiterate and impressionable peasants. Rwanda has an illiteracy rate in the rural areas of 70 percent. RTLM broadcast endless fanatical propaganda urging ordinary citizens to hunt down and kill all Tutsis, whom it described as enemies of democracy, using the familiar epithet *inyenzi* — cockroaches. The radio station played perhaps the most critical role in fomenting and sustaining tension between the two communities by describing the best ways of killing with guns, grenades, *pangas*, clubs, stones, spears, bows and arrows, all of which were played out with deadly results after April 6.

Despite the fact that RTLM was an early target of the RPF advance into Kigali and was bombed out of its studios, it continued to operate until September, when it was finally closed down, broadcasting hate-inspiring untruths from an armoured vehicle which moved into the French-protected zone and then into Zaire with the refugees. It also broadcast destabilizing hate material aimed at increasing tensions in Burundi. RTLM consistently lied about the military advance of the RPF, urging the Hutu population to greater atrocities because, it said, RPF was on the verge of defeat and more help was needed to destroy the Tutsis who were its main support.

Anyone who has heard translations of some of the taped programmes of RTLM will find it difficult to understand why it was not banned from the airwaves as an instrument of ethnic hate and why it took so long to shut it down after the French Operation Turquoise allowed it into southwest Rwanda.

The hatred spread unabashedly by RTLM was not simply government propaganda — that was more Radio Rwanda's style. It was the endless and mindless expression of ethnic cleansing on a scale hitherto unknown in Africa and rarely in the world. To the best of my knowledge, no church leader ever spoke out against RTLM or Radio Rwanda, and some indeed could be heard broadcasting "moments of meditation" over those airwaves prior to April 6. After a while, the endless repetition of lies to an illiterate and poverty-stricken population looking for someone on whom to blame all their woes and with no alternative way of assessing reality becomes truth of a sort, capable of inciting an uncontrollable bloodlust.

An hour after Habyarimana's plane crashed, at 9:30 p.m. on April 6, RTLM broadcast the news of his death, the signal to begin the genocide. Interestingly, the official Radio Rwanda waited — or was forced to wait — until 7:00 the next morning. It is felt that only those who knew exactly what was to be done following the crash would understand the signal from RTLM and begin their bloody work while their victims either were not listening or were waiting for official confirmation from Radio Rwanda.

A whole series of journals and pamphlets was produced to "warn" citizens that the RPF was invading in order to restore the Tutsi monarchy and establish a Tutsi state that would be purged of Hutus — effectively an apartheid state. Rwandese Hutus would be killed or sent to Burundi, while Burundian Tutsis would be welcomed to take over Hutu land in Rwanda. "The Hutu Ten Commandments" (*see appendix*) were widely circulated in extremist newspapers.

Favourite targets of personal morality attacks — a common method used by right-wing propagandists to discredit people — were Prime Minister Uwilingiyimana, Africa's first woman prime minister, because she was an attractive woman, and General Dallaire, a tough-spoken, honest and competent Canadian soldier. But it was radio which did the most damage.

All signs indicate a deliberate and premeditated waging of genocide. Hutu extremists in the CDR faction of the ruling party were motivated by a desire to monopolize power and privilege by eliminating all political opposition. The massacres were planned to destroy the Arusha Accords and derail the peace and democratization process. When Habyarimana was forced, under enormous pressure internationally and regionally, to take a softer line at the April 6 Dar es Salaam summit, he became expendable, and his death was the signal to begin the carnage.

### Awaiting the signal

In sum, orchestrating the logistics of genocide meant misuse of all levels of government and its institutions, as well as the ruling party and its militias. The security forces and the general population were mobilized, encouraged and coerced into joining in the killing. The Presidential Guard and the military were used to train killers and distribute arms. Death lists were circulated to a "Network Zero", and there were countless arbitrary arrests before and during the massacres. The mass media, especially radio, orchestrated ethnic hatred and violence for several years. Weapons, ranging from simple farm implements to sophisticated missiles, were stockpiled and distributed.

By the time the presidential jet was shot down, the situation in Rwanda had become so explosive that the killings began in less than an hour, indicating the level of preparedness for the terror which was to ensue. The exceptional speed with which the genocide began and was almost completed — but for the successful waging of all-out war by the RPF — and the formation of an extremist interim government within 36 hours indicate the extent of the advance planning.

Rwanda's newly appointed president Pasteur Bizimungu blames the UN and the OAU for failing to stop the genocide. He told a meeting on tribal conflicts in the Congolese capital of Brazzaville just before the end of 1994 that the interim government of his country slaughtered a million people in four months due to "indifference from neighbouring states" and that they violated the Universal Declaration of Human Rights "right in front of UN troops who were powerless to do anything because of the gross neglect of the international community".

Bizimungu, a benign, soft-spoken man who wears horn-rimmed glasses and thinks professorially, asked why Africa was able to mobilize so effectively against apartheid but is unable to mobilize against genocide. "Perhaps," he said in an interview I had with him in the presidential mansion where Habyarimana once lived, "it is because blacks were killing blacks in Rwanda and that did not affect your churches in the same way as when whites were oppressing blacks. Does it have something to do with guilt, I wonder, the same way the humanitarianism of your aid agencies eases your consciences?"

The contrast between South Africa's monumental victory over apartheid and Rwandese being hacked to death during the same month is not lost on the politicians in Kigali or church leaders in Nairobi. "While South Africa was preparing for peace and hopefulness in the future, Rwanda was preparing for genocide; and the depressing fact is that we celebrated the one and ignored the other," says Chipenda. "It should serve as a warning about how other struggles may unfold in this next, most dangerous of centuries."

Once known as the country of a thousand hills (*mille collines*), Rwanda is now the country of a million dead, those silent huts and mass graves with skeletal limbs poking through the shallow soil mute testimony to the bloodbath.

A reporter attempting to chronicle these events sees too much horror and knows the first instinct of readers will be to turn away, repelled. The next instinct is to intervene, to do something. But what? Churches, humanitarian agencies motivated by something more than fund-raising and the UN are still struggling with what should have been done before the means, methods and opportunities for genocide were underway.

\* \* \*

In the mountainous region of southeast Rwanda is a small parish called Nyarubuye where, just before April 6, people were tending their fields as they had always done. A young man named Jean-Bosco Mukatwagirimana came home there in July for the first time since he had fled the early slaughters in Kigali, where he worked for an international agency. After three months, his parents' church was still pervaded by the same stench of decay that nauseated me wherever I travelled in those awful days. He could no longer identify his parents, his brothers and sisters, who were somewhere in this grotesquely surreal scene. But he looked carefully and steadily on that moist, warm afternoon after the rains had stopped.

"I cannot even pray for these people," he said to me. "They were our neighbours; so were the killers. I do not understand why they did it. Perhaps I can pray later for my parents and my brothers and sisters but I can never pray for their killers. God will damn them."

# 3. Death and Destruction: The Anatomy of Genocide

Within an hour of the crash of Habyarimana's plane, selective assassination of opposition politicians began in the streets of Kigali. Most of them were Hutu. The first was probably the president of the constitutional court, Joseph Kavaruganda. Contrary to popular belief, concentrated murders during the first days of the atrocities were of Hutu politicians opposed to the self-appointed interim government of Theodore Sindikubwabo and the policies of the extremists he appointed to run the administration of genocide.

## The killing of Agathe Uwilingiyimana

For me, the brutal death of Agathe Uwilingiyamana, the dynamic 41-year-old high school teacher who was Rwanda's acting prime minister when she was butchered about 11 a.m. on April 7 in the United Nations Development Programme (UNDP) compound, symbolizes the utter terror imposed on Kigali and the rest of the country in those first hours.

She was a much-admired moderate Hutu from a peasant family in the area of Butare, where her husband was a university administrator (he was later killed in a separate massacre). Though a moderate leader of the MDR, she was a steadfast opponent of Habyarimana's dictatorial hold on power. When the coalition cabinet was formed in 1992, she became education minister and was made acting prime minister in July 1993.

The sheer terror of her story is a microcosm of the wholesale carnage that swept Kigali right after the plane crash when government officials, clergy, human rights and aid workers and ordinary citizens — Hutu and Tutsi — were hunted down, their bodies strewn a metre or more deep in houses and streets in their tens of thousands.

Mme Uwilingiyamana learned of the plane crash within minutes from General Dallaire. A few hours later she gave a brief interview to Radio France Internationale in which she graphically described her situation: "There is shooting everywhere; people are being terrorized; people are inside my house lying on the floor. We are suffering the consequences of the death of our head of state. We civilians are not to blame for his death."

Early the next morning the Presidential Guard came for her at her residence in the city centre. Panic-stricken, she tried to scale the wall into the home of a consular officer at the US embassy. But the walls were too high, ladders could not be found and the terrified woman's house was surrounded by some twenty Guards. Somehow she found her way through a backyard route to the UNDP, where she felt safe enough to prepare for a broadcast to the nation. Ten Belgian soldiers under UNAMIR command were sent to protect her, but when confronted by the Presidential Guard and ordered to disarm, they did so because they had no mandate from their UNAMIR superiors to resist.

Mme Uwilingiyamana ran for her life and was gunned down at the compound gates before the impotent Belgians. Her blood-stained body lay silent in the road as other UN soldiers huddled in their Hotel Amaharo compound, powerless to act because the morally stunted Security Council in New York, fearful of another debacle like that in Somalia, had ordered Dallaire and his 2500 troops not to use force under any circumstances and to stay in their barracks. Moments later the Presidential Guard, whose hatred and contempt for Belgium was to become legendary, mercilessly tortured the ten soldiers and then summarily executed them.

A zealous crusader for justice who led a long crusade for reconciliation and tolerance between the majority Hutu and minority Tutsi, Mme Uwilingiyamana was equally spirited in her struggle to change Rwandese customs that depicted women as weak and only obedient to men, unfit for public office. In one of her last interviews, holding her four-year-old son on her knee, she told journalists that she refused to say what her ethnic origins were: "I am a Rwandese and I am a person. I have a role to play in my country and it does not matter whether I am a man or a woman, a Hutu or a Tutsi."

After her death, the Forum for African Women's Education (FAWE) expressed its grief at the murder of one of their founding members:

> We must celebrate the life of the great woman, the great African leader that was Agathe Uwilingiyamana. Her recent efforts to reconcile the warring factions, her fight against ethnic interests, her courage in resisting all adversities: these are life-long values that no death can quell. They hold the only hope for Rwanda and for Africa. Long live the spirit of Agathe Uwilingiyamana.

24

## Fleeing "Death City"

Shortly after her death, US marines and Belgian and French paratroopers began a massive airlift of foreigners out of the country. Others were escorted by road to the Burundian capital Bujumbura. Phone lines were soon cut to keep the rest of the world unaware of the extent of the killings; electricity and water supplies were stopped. Kigali took on the air of "Death City", as one Nairobi daily headlined it. Overwhelmed with the wounded, hospitals themselves soon became the site of new massacres as the militias moved in to slaughter people in their beds. As the war heated up, they ceased to function except as displaced persons camps, leaving a small emergency hospital run by ICRC in an old school as the only place for treatment. Nothing else functioned: schools were closed, banks looted, fire trucks wrecked, businesses and government offices smashed. Ragged hotels housed terrified people, but there was no safe place.

Jomo Kenyatta International Airport in Nairobi was soon flooded with expatriates who had fled Rwanda with little more than the clothes on their back. The VIP lounge was opened for embassies to help their traumatized nationals. Diplomats, priests, pastors and nuns, aid and development workers streamed off the planes telling horrific stories of the massacres and their own narrow escapes.

In the chaotic airport at Bujumbura, a 70-year-old nun from Chicoutimi, Quebec, Sister Ghislaine Halley, who had lived in Rwanda for more than 25 years and had been evacuated twice before, told me her story. She had led four elderly colleagues with five orphaned babies through the dark and violent streets of Kigali from their house, which had been attacked by drunken, grenade-throwing youths, to the stadium. There she left them to go in search of help through the nightmare of bombing, shooting and looting. When she arrived at Kigali airport, French troops tried to force her, literally at gunpoint, onto a waiting aircraft to be evacuated to Nairobi.

> I just pushed his gun away — he was a mere boy — and said "*Non, non, non!* I will not leave without my babies and my sisters." I told them to drive me back to the stadium and get them. Those silly men — they were afraid and they refused. But I prayed to God and to our foundress, and finally they sent soldiers with me; and we

drove all the way here through many roadblocks manned by crazy people, with bows and arrows and guns, who wanted to kill me because they thought I might be a Belgian, but when they saw the French they said, "Okay, let her go; she is old and crazy anyway." Now we will go to Chicoutimi and stay until it is over, and then we will come back.

The orphans have since been adopted.

The sight of five aged sisters sitting serenely in the midst of the heat and din and anxiety of Bujumbura's space-age airport terminal, each holding a tiny Rwandese baby on her lap like a protective grandparent, was one of the few signs of hope in the nightmare of those first days.

Most of the evacuees were in shock but their horror was mitigated by their status. At the airport in Nairobi the US even set up a desk to process the dogs and cats that emerged from handbags and purses.

There were no Rwandese aboard the European, American and Canadian transport planes.

Back in Rwanda maids and security guards, drivers and office workers, colleagues at NGOs were left to fend for themselves and their families and died in their thousands. Parents who begged UNAMIR soldiers to evacuate their children were told that the orders were clear: do not evacuate any Rwandese.

"I had to make choices. We couldn't take our domestics and we could only bring one bag each so I brought my cats in my purse," a distraught French woman and her son told me on April 9.

Rwandese survivors are bitter about how quickly and efficiently more than 5000 foreigners were evacuated. French troops literally fought their way into town, collected their nationals and fought their way back to the airport, where they forced the Presidential Guard to remove fire trucks barricading the runway to prevent evacuation flights from landing. But there was no help for terrified Rwandese from the foreign soldiers or the toothless UNAMIR.

To be sure, President Habyarimana's widow and 15 members of her immediate family were within hours on a flight to Paris, where they were guests of France's presidential family, to whom they had been personally close. It was different for ordinary people without friends in the Elysée Palace. Eye-witnesses described a Rwandese woman being hauled along a street by several young men with machetes. As they tore at her clothes, she looked at the UN troops with their blue berets worn at a jaunty angle in a terrified, desperate hope that they could save her from the slow, agonizing death facing her. But no one moved. "It's not in our mandate. We are forbidden," said one of them leaning against his jeep, the rain spattering his camou-flaged flak jacket.

## UNAMIR — spectators of genocide

The 2500 UNAMIR troops led by General Dallaire had their hands tied by their political masters in New York where, under UN rules, Rwanda's self-appointed government of killers held a seat on the UN Security Council until September when it was replaced by the new government. The foreign troops were forced to be spectators of a genocide which they had known for months in advance was in the making. UNAMIR's role was defined as that of observer to the "made in Africa" peace deal, responsible only to monitor the ceasefire in the north of the country and oversee multi-party elections.

Even before Habyarimana's plane crashed, Boutros-Ghali had been threatening to withdraw the UNAMIR troops. He and his UN bureaucrats had rejected a plan developed by Dallaire much earlier to "neutralize" the main killers: the Presidential Guard, the gendarmerie and the worst of the *interahamwe*.

"We could have taken them out within 48 hours and saved thousands of lives, but New York said no," journalists were told by a clearly frustrated Dallaire, the trim, no-nonsense Canadian professional soldier who commanded the tiny force until Sep-tember, usually wearing a flak jacket and sleeping on a folding cot in his office at a former tourist hotel. "If we had been able to deploy the troops and equipment with a mandate to prevent these crimes against humanity, I believe we could have curtailed the killings. We could not have stopped it all, but I think we could have saved hundreds of thousands of lives".

On April 21 the Security Council further tarnished its already dismal record by voting to reduce Dallaire's force from 2500 to 270 troops. In fact, 450 stayed. Frustrated by their token presence and flaccid mandate, these Ghanaians, Zimbabweans, Malians, Senegalese and Canadians spent most of their time trying to negotiate temporary ceasefires between the FAR and the RPF to allow evacuation of thousands of terrified civilians locked in two Catholic churches and a hotel in downtown Kigali.

Dallaire, I believe, interpreted his mandate as broadly as possible, but it was almost hopeless. The April 21 vote restricted him to co-ordinating humanitarian aid, transferring civilians to safe zones when he could get a brief temporary ceasefire and negotiating cessations of hostilities, which would be agreed upon over and over and then promptly violated.

Most Rwandese leaders who survived the holocaust say the UN should have immediately widened Dallaire's mandate to protect civilians, supplying him with more soldiers and equipment. Indeed, even by the time the war ended and Dallaire was returning to Canada, he had only 3000 of the promised 5500 mainly African peacekeeping troops.

## The UN's failures

Some of the harshest criticisms of those first weeks of the genocide are reserved for the UN secretary general and his special representative. It was their unreliable reports, arguably biased on behalf of the illegitimate regime, on which the Council based its April 21 resolution. Both insisted that the problem was Hutus killing Tutsis and Tutsis killing Hutus and a "civil war" between the so-called interim government and the RPF. They did not condemn or for that matter even mention the blatantly genocidal policies of Sindikubwabo's regime. Boutros-Ghali openly followed the French line that the killings started when the RPF battalion broke out of its compound in Kigali the morning after Habyarimana's death to fight the Presidential Guard in the streets and RPF troops began moving from bases in the north. RPF would argue from April 7 until it drove the interim government from the country on July 4 that the only way to stop the killings and protect civilians was to replace the rulers. Stretching credibility to the breaking point, the UN continued to give *de facto* recognition to the self-appointed government, although everyone knew that it was covered in blood, ruling illegally and in the hands of extremists committed to the Hutu ideology.

Booh-Booh, the special representative, even argued that the biggest obstacle in trying to negotiate the numerous ceasefires was the RPF's refusal to recognize the Sindikubwabo government. To others who watched his futile efforts, this was carrying neutrality to the point of absurdity in the face of clear evidence of genocide — based among other things on public statements by the president and members of the interim government continuing to call on the people to kill. Whether or not he was incompetent, as some have charged, Booh-Booh, who was eventually recalled, was clearly carrying out orders calling for a ceasefire and recognition of the discredited interim administration — which meant in essence a recognition of genocide.

By April 21, Rwanda had been abandoned by the international community. All embassies were closed and staff evacuated. Humanitarian organizations left. Opposition politicians and leaders were dead, except for a few who escaped into exile. An essentially fascist government was calling the shots. The UN was at best ineffective. The international community's moral vacuum and an almost deafening silence from churches attested to a paralysis that was in stark contrast to the hyperactive though unproductive involvement of European powers in Bosnia. Indeed, all through the Rwandese conflict, the UN was preoccupied with what Boutros-Ghali once called "the rich man's war" in the former Yugoslavia.

From the moment word arrived in Nairobi of Habyarimana's death, the AACC began to pressure its member churches and its partners around the world to bring all possible attention of the international community to the issues of justice, peace and reconciliation in the Rwandese situation. The AACC was also a part of the international ecumenical body formed to co-ordinate humanitarian assistance, community development, peace and reconciliation and communications called Church World Action-Rwanda (CWA-R), which was established by the Lutheran World Federation and the World Council of Churches and has raised some US$21 million since April 6.

Often paralyzed by problems, the Organization for African Unity was in the forefront of change in the case of Rwanda. The OAU had brokered many of the deals leading up to the Arusha Accords and had monitors observing the ceasefire. Perennially strapped for resources, it could do little more after April 6 than issue statements which were, on the whole, more outspoken than those of the UN. OAU secretary general Salim Ahmed Salim of Tanzania condemned the "wanton killings" on April 8 and repeated his message to both sides to end hostilities. After the UN's craven pullout, he expressed disappointment that Rwanda had been abandoned and suggested that once again Africa was suffering from indifference, due this time to the UN's preoccupation with Bosnia. After strong representations from Salim and others in Africa, the Security Council began in mid-May to consider developing UNAMIR-II as an effort to end the genocide.

Despite strenuous efforts by the interim government, the OAU, at its annual meeting in Tunis in June, condemned the systematic killings and called for war crimes trials and a cessation of hostilities. Ironically, however, the OAU seated the self-appointed Rwandese government — in violation, some members argued, of its own charter.

However, as the slaughter of Tutsis escalated after the first days in which mostly opposition Hutus were targetted, a curious malaise settled over the international community. Even when 40,000 corpses floated in a single day down the Kagera River from Rwanda into Lake Victoria, world organizations had difficulty responding. Even when 250,000 Rwandese fled in 24 hours across the borders into camps in western Tanzania, the UN could not act except to offer humanitarian aid in the Benaco camps. No one outside was calling for direct intervention that might put an end to the killing fields. However troubled they might be at what was going on, Western nations offered little more than expressions of sympathy for the victims and shock at the images of bloated bodies doing a bizarre dance of death in the swirling waters of Rusumo Falls at the Tanzania-Rwanda border.

Many of these bodies were of women and children, some decapitated. I saw the body of one woman floating in the river, with a dead child tied to each arm. Better to drown than face the raging militias.

## Leisurely diplomacy

On May 17, six weeks after the carnage began, the UN reversed its earlier decision to let Rwanda suffer on its own and decided to send 5500 peacekeepers, mainly from Africa, back to Rwanda. There were expressions of incredulity at the Kigali compound where the tiny UNAMIR remnant hunkered down under nightly mortar and artillery duels. Who would provide all these troops? Where would the vehicles and armoured personnel carriers and weapons and food and tents and communications equipment and logistics and air transport come from? Who would put the plans in place? It was a logistical nightmare which, due to UN inaction, was fortunately delayed for weeks, and in a sense never really happened.

Sanctions were instituted, but they had no bite since weapons were coming in unhindered from the usual arms merchants via Zaire. Moreover, by this time Rwanda was so destitute and starving and war-torn that very little further damage could be done to the economy.

Special envoys shuttled around Africa. The World Food Programme and ICRC pleaded for safe zones to be established and protected by the UN so that food could at least be distributed, but nothing much happened except that thousands continued to be killed. Many more died of hunger, disease and wounds, while the fortunate ones fled to neighbouring countries and the violent and uncertain life of refugee camps.

About a month after independent observers began referring to the massacres as genocide, the US State Department admitted that it was out of ideas and that few people in the US supported doing anything to end the bloodshed. "We don't have any plan. We have to hope that these people will eventually stop killing each other. They cannot kill each other forever."

When the Security Council approved sending 5500 UNAMIR-II troops to keep the peace and help Rwanda rebuild itself, the war was far from over. The RPF insisted that as long as the extremists were in power — in Kigali, then in Gitarama, later in Gisenyi — they would fight for a military victory as the only way of ending the extermination of Rwandese. The US insisted on a ceasefire before making any firm commitments.

On June 18, a month after "authorizing" the 5500 peacekeepers, the Security Council passed another resolution "deploying" the troops. The US, which did not want another Somalia, threatened to veto any resolution that would insert peacekeepers prior to decisions about how they would operate.

Then there was the question of logistics. Who would supply equipment and how would it get to landlocked Rwanda, a thousand kilometres from the nearest port? Only the US had the capability to launch such a logistical operation. But Rwanda was not Iraq. It has no oil, and its global significance was minimal.

Dallaire had by now developed an operational plan, and a reconnaissance team had drawn up a list of needs and locations, especially for communications. But the US continued to drag its feet. There was a disgraceful dispute over the terms under which the US would supply the UN fifty armoured personnel carriers which Dallaire, who had only two at the time, urgently needed to evacuate civilians trapped in two Kigali churches. While this dispute was going on, two massacres were committed at St Andrew's College, killing 250 Tutsis and six priests. A direct appeal to UNAMIR by two expatriate priests elicited an emotional outburst from the UN spokesperson, Canadian Major Jean-Guy Plante: "We cannot do a goddam thing. We have no men and no equipment to go and evacuate these people. It hurts me to say this but it's true."

It became apparent that any US involvement in Rwanda, other than flying in troops from 14 different African countries, would not be under the command of Dallaire or the UN. The United States wanted to orchestrate its own operations, and refused to relinquish control to the UN. It preferred for a time to concentrate on its own rather dangerous, but highly telegenic, air drops of supplies on refugee concentrations in Zaire.

During the same Security Council debate in mid-June, objections were raised to the use of the term "genocide" for what was happening in Rwanda, because under international law UN members would then be obliged to do something to stop it. Better to call these incidents "massacres" or "slaughters" or some other euphemism. As diplomacy continued on its leisurely course during May and June more hundreds of thousands of people were dying. Oxfam UK now set the death toll at one million; and others said it was even higher. Probably no one will ever know definitely. Africans are not accustomed to keeping the kind of meticulous records the Nazis did in the last Holocaust. Finally, on July 1, just three days before an RPF victory ended the war, US secretary of state Warren Christopher told the Senate that "it is clear there has been a genocide which should be punished by an international court".

## Blaming the Tutsis

Within the country the government of April 8 had quickly consolidated its plan to eliminate all forms of opposition and began painting the retroactive scenario of a planned Tutsi takeover by the RPF. It presented itself as legitimate, although its 19-member cabinet contained only MRND and CDR members, and claimed to be in control of the country, although it evacuated to Gitarama already on April 12, once the fighting for Kigali intensified.

Just after the French launched Operation Turquoise on June 23, setting up a so-called protected zone in southwest Rwanda, I interviewed Andre Ntagerura, the interim government's minister of transport and communications at Cyangugu. He had been a long-serving member of Habyarimana's cabinet, a member of the central committee of MRND and a shareholder in Radio RTLM. The interview took place less than ten days before Rwanda fell to the RPF. He is now in Zaire.

The interview was hastily arranged in the office of Emmanuel Bagambiki, the Cyangugu prefect, a notorious hardliner who is alleged to have organized massacres in 1992 and 1993. Both men were unrepentant although the RPF was closing in on all sides and they knew that their only protection came from French Legionnaires and paratroopers.

Some of the most intensive massacres in Rwanda occurred in Cyangugu city, on lovely turquoise-coloured Lake Kivu, not far from Bukavu in Zaire. Of the some 55,000 Tutsis who lived here prior to the civil war, fewer than 8000 survived, and when I visited their ICRC camp, the survivors were in a pitiful condition. In the space of a single day we were shown eleven mass graves, some already exposed by the wind and rain, others obviously quite fresh.

Survivors told dreadful stories of their ordeal, especially in the city stadium, where they were regularly subjected to attacks by fragmentation grenades. They said the prefect had organized the entire slaughter beginning on April 9.

Still fearful of attacks by the *interahamwe*, the survivors were living in blue and green plastic-sheeted huts provided by

ICRC on the side hills of a tea plantation about 10 kilometres from Cyangugu at a place called Nyarushishi, just below the local headquarters of Operation Turquoise. They were gaunt and badly traumatized.

Daniel Kamatali, a retired electrician, told me that there had been more than 450,000 Tutsis in the prefecture. "All of them who are left are here now. I was hiding in a church with my wife and five children when they came for us on April 27. My wife and two children were killed. I heard them shouting to 'cut us down to size' because Tutsis were too tall for their own good. They slashed me here and here."

Trembling with anxiety, the 58-year-old man lifted his ragged trouser leg to show a brutal scar across his Achilles tendon. His nose was still covered with a bandage. He can no longer walk without crutches and his nose was still badly infected. He survived because "they did not kill all of us on that occasion. I don't know why, I wish they had because even now no one cares enough about Tutsis to help."

Another survivor was Calixte Karangwa, a labourer who lost his family of seven:

> Young *interahamwe* did the killing but they were helped by local police. They used hoes and clubs to hack about 100 of us to death. It took a very long time, and twice they became so tired they had to rest from their work. I was injured but managed to hide behind some bushes while they were resting. When it became dark I got away, but I left my children behind, for which I feel very bad now, but I am sure they were all killed.

Our first questions to Ntagerura were about the massacres in Cyangugu. Angrily dismissing the reports as RPF propaganda, he said that only a few were killed and they "deserved" what happened to them.

> They are responsible because the RPF resumed fighting after the president's plane was shot down and people began killing each other. There is nothing our government could do to stop the killing because all our soldiers were busy fighting the RPF.

The minister and prefect sat behind a table covered by a freshly pressed white table cloth. Both wore well-cut blue suits, gleaming white shirts and smart ties. A coloured print of Habyarimana in full uniform still hung on the wall.

You know about apartheid? You know how a few whites dominated all the Bantu? Well, that is the same here. We are 90 percent Hutu, but 10 percent Tutsis — the English-speaking RPF — want to dominate everything. That is apartheid, and we must stamp it out.

Both men insisted that the RPF had actually committed more massacres than the militias.

When our president was preparing for peace, the RPF was preparing for war. We want peace but they killed our president. All we have done is defend our country. We believe in democracy. Ask the French colonel. He will tell you.

The interview was abruptly terminated because a cabinet meeting had been called suddenly at a nearby hotel. When we left the prefect's office, we found that gendarmes under control of these "democrats" had arrested our Burundian driver, a Tutsi, and taken him away. We made a complaint to the colonel, who had just received three military helicopters carrying French defence minister François Léotard, an entourage of French television journalists and a supply of chilled white wine and roast chicken. Léotard, eager for good coverage of the controversial French operation, offered us food and ordered Colonel Didier Thibeault to have our driver released. By the time we returned to the prefecture, the terrified driver had been taken to a cell where he was being beaten. Thibeault's tough-looking paratroopers, based in Toulouse, told us this was their fourth intervention in Africa.

"We know what to do with these Africans. You just talk tough. Watch." Col. Etienne Jacques, his tricolours flying, stormed into the prefect's office, pounded on the desk and walked out without a backward glance. "Your driver will be released to me. I will guarantee his safety. I will now escort you to the border post."

* * *

Wherever I travelled in Kigali or the countryside during April, May and June, three recurring images came to haunt me.

Because we had to drive away from the main roads to avoid the army and militias, who did not take kindly to journalists exposing their activities, we criss-crossed Rwanda's lush rolling hills on rutted back roads — often speeding through small villages. One always knew where there had been a massacre by the sickeningly sweet smell of rotting corpses hanging over the area like an invisible cloud.

These villages were so uncharacteristic of Africa because they were deserted, deathly still. The only sign of human presence was the intimate, personal debris: mounds of brightly coloured clothes lying in the dust where they had been dropped by people running from the militias, who were "roaring like hyenas", survivors told us; hundreds of coloured snapshots, curled and bent and blowing in the hot wind, photographs of baptisms and weddings and funerals and feasts and first communions; certificates of some mechanical skill or other; letters and bills; all the bits and pieces of stuff that people, even poor people, accumulate and treasure. Pieces of their whole lives lay there in front of wrecked and looted houses from which even the windows and door frames had been carried off. But there was never anyone around. There are always people in African villages, walking on the roads, sitting in the shade, chatting and bartering in the markets. Villages are a colourful and noisy beehive of activity. In Rwanda there was no one anywhere in those evil months. Deserted.

Almost deserted. Roving packs of fat brown dogs seemed everywhere. At night, their howling and barking was a constant reminder that they were feasting on the dead. During the day they ran silently through the empty villages. African dogs are not pets: they are usually thin and sullen, watching alertly for any scrap. In Rwanda during the war they became vicious. In Kigali they eventually had to be shot, we were told, because eating human flesh made them attack humans. "They have become like cannibals who have developed a taste for human flesh," a soldier said.

In all, the vicious war lasted for 102 days. Kigali fell to the RPF on July 4 and Gisenyi on July 17. A new government led by two Hutus and one Tutsi was formed on July 19. Nearly a million people had been killed, about three million were refugees and another two million were internally displaced. Africa's most densely populated country had become a ghost state.

The plan to exterminate Tutsis and opposition Hutus and to implicate every surviving person in the genocide was almost a complete success. The massacres were systematic: entire families were hunted down, women raped, children and babies targetted, killings of everyone done in the most appalling mental and physical torment without distinction — priests, nuns, pastors, evangelists, journalists, lawyers, doctors, academics, teachers, nurses and ordinary women and men.

It was a hell.

# 4. Inside and Outside: How People Survived

In the face of genocide, some people in Rwanda rose to heights of courage and compassion that make the human spirit soar with hope. Many laid down their lives for their sisters and brothers, regardless of their ethnicity. Others proved to be craven cowards who betrayed family and friends and joined the frenzy of killings simply in order to stay alive for one more day. Most just managed to survive, demonstrating yet again amid such horrible situations and conditions the astounding resilience of Africans in the face of adversities too awful for most to absorb, let alone comprehend.

Rwanda, the country of a thousand hills, now also has a thousand stories. Brigadier Henry Anyidoho, the Ghanaian deputy commander of UNAMIR who became a kind of mentor and friend, says it is also a country of a thousand lies. He should know: it was his thankless job to spend many hours trying to negotiate ceasefires which would then allow him to evacuate terrified Rwandese hiding from their killers. More than once, he and his troops were almost killed when one side or the other fired on the canvas-covered lorries with their blue flags and red crosses flying, killing helpless women and children who thought they were safe.

## The banality of evil

There are stories of survival within the country under the most harrowing of conditions — in Kigali and in the country-side. There are stories from enormous unorganized camps of displaced where people tried to survive, with food aid coming sometimes once a month, and marauders lurking in the unharvested fields of tall sorghum. There are stories beyond number of massacres and of survivors. There are stories of war.

There are also stories from outside the country. Many stories have been told by CNN and BBC about the largest refugee camp in the world, which appeared within 24 hours at an obscure place called Ngara in the dry western hills of Tanzania. And then there is Goma, in eastern Zaire, where tourists used to come and volcanoes burn red at night, which became the world's symbol of desperation and helplessness for a few weeks. Here gigantic Russian Antonovs dropped like stones onto battered runways to bring tons of rice and beans and white four-wheel drive vehicles and plastic sheets and sometimes beer.

There are also personal stories, most of which will never be told because there is no one left to tell them except maybe late at night in mind-bending dreams and shuddering nightmares.

There are stories of people going mad from grief and fear. Once in Goma, my Zairean friend and I were on the back of a truck on a road clogged with misery, trying not to gag at the stench of the corpses wrapped in straw mats and piled like logs of wood on the black lava rock, when we saw a woman dancing along in front of us, stark naked and screaming endlessly.

These are also stories of children brought into the Red Cross hospital in the centre of Kigali with their ears cut off and their sweet faces slashed, their hands and feet missing, bodies covered in gauze. Weary nurses would drop little mounds of beans into their mouths like mother birds while mortars crashed just outside, fired by — who knows?

Stories, too, horrid, frantic stories, of what Hannah Arendt called in her book *Eichmann in Jerusalem* "the banality of evil". I became fixated on this observation for a while, especially when I interviewed Marie at a makeshift RPF jail in a battered town called Kabuga. Marie had killed her godmother, or maybe it was her stepmother, and two of her friends with a *mazu*, a nail-studded club. She told us quite frankly all about it, twisting a small blue ring honouring the Virgin Mary. She was sorry, "but they made me do it, and I loved that woman like my own mother, but she was already badly wounded". Marie was sad, but the alternative had been her own death and perhaps that of her children — a moral choice few of us would want to have thrust on us.

An elderly man in the same jail had "finished off" his badly battered older brother because they told him to. After they left, he jumped into a pit latrine full of faeces up to his neck to hide. He would have drowned or died except that after three days someone came to use it and heard his feeble cries and rescued him. But it turned out to be his brother's wife. She turned him over to the RPF and he went to jail.

Major Plante of UNAMIR was driving one day near Nyanza close to Gitarama in central Rwanda when he came across 25 corpses recently slaughtered and piled by the road. He stopped to take down some details when he thought he heard a little whimper. Legs and arms were sticking out of the bloody jumble at grotesque angles but somewhere in that pile of horror someone was alive. It was a baby, about three months old, and the soldiers rescued her, deep under people who may have been her parents. Plante is an eloquent and rather profane military policeman in his mid-50s from St Bruno, Quebec, who came to Rwanda from Somalia. Telling this story, his eyes moisten and he starts showing pictures of his own grandchildren in Canada.

There are many stories of people whose lives were saved for strange reasons: people who begged to be killed and were told by the militias, "We are too tired; we have been killing all day"; people like Josephine, who were hacked into unconsciousness and lay among the decomposing bodies, forgotten by the killers; people who hid in ceilings and sewers and latrines and storehouses and watched in horror and helplessness as their spouses and children were murdered.

The brother of a friend was trying to escape from his hunters with a few relatives. He pushed them across a road quickly, into the bush, but as he moved behind them, he was caught. They began questioning him, looked at the Tutsi designation on his identification card and told him to prepare to die. "What is your last wish before we kill you?", they asked teasingly and beat him a little. "I am a Christian, I wish to pray." He got down on his knees, closed his eyes and began to pray. "I heard one of them say, 'Let's get it over with, hurry!'. But another one said, 'This man is crazy down there on his knees. Let him go.' And they did." Survival? A miracle?

On the streets of Goma one day, when cholera was sweeping through like a mediaeval plague, I witnessed a small personal slice of the tragedy. Out on the wide, incredibly dusty boulevard where people streamed by looking for anywhere to rest their exhausted, emaciated bodies, a woman was lying on the hard ground, dysentery cramps wracking her whole system. A man, perhaps her husband, stood over her. Sometimes he bent and pulled her dress down to cover her thin limbs, an act of kindness and modesty in a place where, even in extreme illness, modesty is important. He crouched beside her and said something in her ear, but she could not respond. He smoothed her clothing again, her body twitched spasmodically and she died. He stood, covered her face, looked at her for a while and then walked away towards the lake, wherever the other refugees were going.

**Searching for survivors**

Rwandese colleagues on the staff of the AACC lived through those ghastly times with no news of their families. If they went home, they were likely to be killed, because the death squads especially targetted intellectuals and professionals, about 90 percent of whom lost their lives if they were unable to flee to nearby countries. André Karamaga, a Swiss-educated Presbyterian theologian, finally got home in July to find out that his father had been killed at Kabgayi, the huge Roman Catholic centre which served the entire country with schools, hospital, dispensary, cathedral, seminary, religious orders and large properties. More than 30,000 Tutsis sought sanctuary there, and many were killed. Altogether, Karamaga had 28 members of his immediate family — brothers and sisters, nephews and nieces, aunts and uncles — massacred. He has adopted three of his family's orphaned children.

Mike Rugema, who worked in the refugee and emergency services department at AACC and is now a Rwandese diplomat, was highly vocal in Nairobi, warning of genocide long before it was accepted. He told me that 50 members of his family, including grandparents and grandchildren, lost their lives. He now has 11 orphans in his family, aged six months to 13 years. "Yet I am considered lucky, and indeed I am. In many families, there were no survivors to tell the tale. Close to 100 people perished in my home village, where entire families — and families are large in Rwanda were wiped out."

Another good friend, Jean-Bosco Kimenyi Mukulira, who teaches French at AACC's Communications Training Centre, waited throughout the long days and weeks to get married, not knowing what members of his family would survive eventually to attend the ceremony. When he arrived in Kigali soon after the war ended his worst fears were realized: his parents, brothers, sisters, their spouses and their children — more than 20 — were all dead.

Travelling in and out of Rwanda during the war, I always carried lists of names to search for. Rarely could the people be found. Most as it turned out were already dead; others I would hear about and bring back slightly hopeful news, only to learn on the next trip they had been caught and killed.

Julienne Munyaneza is a Rwandese woman who works in London for the World Association for Christian Communication (WACC). Her husband, Malachie Munyaneza, is a Presbyterian pastor. He and their four young children were in Rwanda when the holocaust began. Twice I almost found him, only to be told that he had moved on a few days earlier. For weeks Julienne sat by her phone, desperate for word of her children. A few days after the war ended, she flew into Kigali and found them all, thin, ill and in pain from the endless walking, hiding, tension and lack of food, but alive. They are in Britain now but already the young pastor is ready to come home.

## Genocide is no accident

Each of these many stories has a context. The massacres inside Rwanda and what happened outside in the camps were not accidents of war, in which civilians get caught in the crossfire — horrific and unacceptable in a world we had hoped was becoming more humane, but still a circumstance of war. The massive exodus of refugees swarming into Tanzania, Zaire and to some extent Burundi was not just the upheaval of a people fleeing for their lives, which we have become all too accustomed to seeing on television. It was policy. The killings and the refugee crisis were planned. Whether people survived murderous militias in church compounds or disease and hunger in squalid refugee camps, they were human pawns in a deadly political game whose goal was, and still is, the retention of power by extremists bent on shaping Rwanda to suit their own twisted ideology.

Unfortunately, the international community was an unwitting and naive accomplice of the former government's policies, reacting as it did to demands by people who watched the soul-searing television coverage that something be done, anything — except committing an international force to stop the massacres and head off the refugee exodus. The US was negative to this idea and there was little enthusiasm for it in the UN Security Council. Positive calls for action to bring about justice and to impose peace to make it possible were overwhelmed by conventional wisdom that the situation was too violent and confused and that a clear outcome was not immediately in sight.

The French, for their own dubious ulterior motives, did take humanitarian action, but its effect was to buy time for the government of genocide to organize the exodus of Hutus, along with its army, militias, politicians, functionaries, their families, their cars, buses and possessions, Rwanda's hard currency and gold reserves. The former government saw this rout not as a defeat but as a strategic withdrawal to gain time to rebuild before returning to finish the genocide. The RPF was faced with a bankrupt, depopulated, frightened and traumatized population with none of the infrastructure of government in place. The camps became squalid concentrations of hatred and frustration, with much of the population once again prisoners of the old regime.

It was a clever, if diabolical, plan, and it remains to be seen if it will work. The agony of it all is, as some evaluations of the emergencies programme are beginning to suggest, that the relief agencies and the UN High Commissioner for Refugees were unable to avoid the trap cynically set for them by the extremists. Those who set a policy of massacring their own people knew they could rely on international relief agencies, including those of Protestant, Catholic and evangelical churches in Europe and North America, to respond with an enormous effort to alleviate the massive suffering forced on Rwandese by their self-appointed government and its allies, particularly in Zaire.

**The flight to Tanzania**

Within hours of the arrival of 250,000 refugees swarming into a remote corner of rural Tanzania in early May, the UNHCR was describing it as the "biggest, most gigantic wave of refugees ever seen". The mass media were flooded with superlatives (the Benaco Camp was called, incorrectly, "the biggest refugee camp in history") and with images of a quagmire of miserable humanity drinking foul water and sleeping in the open as corpses floated past in the nearby river. People were even alleged to have been eaten by lions.

There is no doubt that the calamity was of apocalyptic proportions and that people were petrified of the advancing RPF army, which had by then taken about half the country. "If Tutsis catch you, they slit your skin from head to foot and skin you alive," said one refugee. In fact, aid workers fishing bodies from the swollen Kagera River reported that the corpses bore the same brutal wounds as those inflicted on people slashed to death in churches inside Rwanda.

It became clear that many of the refugees had heard of atrocities committed by RPF but had not themselves witnessed them. RPF soldiers certainly committed many revenge killings, but the refugees were victims of a mass hysteria whipped up by the interim government. It also became clear that members of the professional *interahamwe* had crossed over with the refugees. Even so, the emergency co-ordinators (UNHCR) concentrated for a long time on setting up camps and food distribution systems. Only when it was too late did agencies begin complaining that well-organized and known killers had taken over the camp structures and consolidated power. The UNHCR, proud that the refugees were organized in exactly the same commune structure as in Rwanda, guaranteed that the same extremists continued to hold power in their Tanzanian sanctuary.

Although hundreds of thousands of people had already died in Rwanda, the "humanitarian emergency" in Tanzania immediately overshadowed the genocide and diverted world attention from the internal cause of the exodus, injustice. At best this was naive; at worst, it verged on collusion with killers. Precisely the same people who planned and implemented the policy of massacres now had control of Benaco. Some of the agency workers and volunteers who flooded into Tanzania even stated that their job was only to feed people, not to ask if they had killed anyone.

And the massacres continued. The niceties of the definition of genocide continued to be debated in the hallowed halls of the UN while thousands literally starved to death and survivors will be scarred for life, physically and emotionally. At the end of 1994, the Tanzanian camps, well-organized and still receiving guests, show no signs of being dismantled and the Rwanda government has huge hostile encampments on its borders.

Although some agencies recognized the trap, the same mistake was astonishingly repeated on a much larger scale two months later in Zaire, where a rump government, complete with lots of hard currency which legally belongs inside Rwanda, is in charge, training soldiers to wage guerilla and conventional war and maintaining a reign of terror over ordinary citizens. By the end of 1994 the camps in Zaire had become extremely dangerous. Aid agencies, warning that their relief operations were "untenable", expressed outrage at having become "unwilling accomplices" to massive human rights abuses.

Naive humanitarianism has not worked in the Rwanda crisis, if it ever worked anywhere. I began my career as a foreign correspondent by covering the 1968 Nigeria-Biafra civil war, in which a million people died of starvation. In retrospect, the action of relief agencies, in that case led by churches, prolonged the war, contributing to further suffering from which Nigeria has never fully recovered. Twenty-five years later, we seem to have learned little.

This is not to denigrate the assistance that emergency aid brings to victims, nor the basic human decency of people the world over who believe that the hungry should be fed and the sick healed and widows comforted and orphans cared for. But beyond those basic instincts, as Chipenda has stated again and again, the concern for justice must permeate every action by churches; and justice involves looking at the murky political issues which cause massacres and refugee exoduses and denouncing injustice without taking partisan positions. It seems in the case of Rwanda that de-politicized emergency aid is easier than long range initiatives for justice, peace and reconciliation.

## Holy Family Church

While life in the camps is squalid, violent, tenuous and hopeless, nothing can approach the sheer terror of the places people congregated for sanctuary inside Rwanda. There are certain survival techniques in the camps and orphanages, but survival within the country seemed almost solely a matter of caprice.

In the Catholic compound at Nyamata some 15,000 people died in the extensive network of buildings. The metal ceiling looked like a sieve, so extensive was the damage from fragmentation grenades. Blood and body parts were everywhere. The large baptismal font contained a tiny corpse, and the priests' vestments, hanging in the sacristy, bore bloody hand-prints. In a nearby classroom a white Jesus standing with his lambs is painted like a mural on the wall. Below this pastoral scene, the body of what appeared to be a teenager remained after the other bodies had been buried in a mass grave nearby, his face contorted in a fearful grin. As I gazed at this painfully poignant image through the lens of my camera, I thought again of Josephine's words: "the angels have left us."

One of the haunting things about a situation like Rwanda is the gruesome repetition of events. One of my most numbing experiences was at a slightly sinister-looking red brick church squatting malevolently in the centre of Kigali, to which I returned several times in both war and peace, obsessed with a need to know what went on inside for about three months and what was happening now that some peace had been realized. Eglise Sainte Famille — Holy Family Church — has achieved a special kind of notoriety even in a country where many church buildings were slaughterhouses. Somehow people survived here, although to the frightened inmates it was a place of evil.

Shortly after the presidential jet crashed, about 8000 Tutsis living in Kigali sought safety in the main church and its many out-buildings, where they became victims of a sinister game of cat-and-mouse. They were the mice in the hands of a wicked priest and a fanatical woman leader of the *interahamwe*, who promised to look after refugees while in fact finding ways to have them killed.

UNAMIR laboriously negotiated several ceasefires to evacuate some of these refugees to safe zones held by the RPF. A few succeeded; others ended in failure and disaster. Inside the main church, whose huge wooden doors seemed always to be shut and padlocked, conditions were appalling. There was little food and water. People were packed under pews and behind the altar and jammed into tiny rooms, filthy and terrified of the raging militias outside, always ready to strike. Almost daily, people were abducted and killed while horrified inmates of this death church helplessly watched machete-wielding *interahamwe* do their deadly work.

The second time I went to the church was on June 3, in a UNAMIR convoy led by Brigadier Anyidoho. The first time, in May, our convoy had been attacked en route, and we had to return, leaving the refugees helpless in their ordeal. About

10:00 on a sunny Friday morning, an armoured personnel carrier (in which three journalists cowered) and five canvas-covered lorries sped through the silent, empty streets, past the bombed-out buildings. Artillery and mortar-fire were belching noise and smoke — in order, we decided, to let UNAMIR know that this latest ceasefire was tenuous at best.

When we arrived, about 500 people were lined up outside in the compound in two groups, pitiful, small belongings clutched in their hands. Many of the women had small babies on their backs. They looked scared, though hopeful, but strangely passive. They were dirty and very thin. The smaller group wanted to go to the FAR-controlled zone; the larger to Kabuga, a suburb of Kigali already "liberated" by the RPF.

We could see the militias circling around the roads next to the compound. Senior officers of the FAR and gendarmerie stood around talking to the UNAMIR officers, but our attention was riveted to a handsome man in his mid-30s with a portable loud-hailer and a pistol on his hip. As he walked around reading out names from a list, a heavy-set woman wearing a camouflage jacket double-checked every name. She grew clearly more agitated as it became evident that the vast majority of evacuees wanted to go to Kabuga.

These two people had become notorious. Father Wenceslas Munyeshyaka was the parish priest at the huge 60-year-old church. His companion was Odette Nyirabagenzi, a member of the CDR, the fanatical Hutu extremist wing of the MRND. According to *African Rights* reports, she was "personally responsible for the deaths of countless people".

As we three journalists went around taking pictures and trying to interview evacuees, it became obvious that these two were enraged by the whole exercise but could do little as long as we and UNAMIR were around. We heard the epithet *inyenzi* (cockroach) repeated endlessly. Few people would talk to us in French, and those who did made certain the priest and militia leader could not see them talking to us. They seemed less afraid of government soldiers or gendarmes. "We are very hungry," they told us. "There is no food. Caritas [the Catholic relief agency] gets here only once in a while. It is not safe here. Those militias up there [pointing to the road] kill us and beat us up. Help us escape please."

Odette Nyirabagenzi angrily refused to speak to us, but Fr Wenceslas launched into a diatribe about the RPF bombing the compound. There were holes in the rectory roof and over the sanctuary part of the church.

"We've been hit 14 times. No, it's not safe. The RPF bombs us all, but it is killing its own people [Tutsis] here and the people who live in this commune are very angry. I don't really blame them, although I try to help everyone — Hutu and Tutsi — because we know everyone. The problem is not as simple as you international journalists say it is. It is a problem like apartheid. The minority wants to regain power, so it is political. We just want the war to end and send the RPF back where it came from. If they had not started the war all this death would have ended a long time ago. We have to stop the war before anything can happen."

He reluctantly posed for a few pictures and went through his list again as people clambered onto the lorries, assisted by the UNAMIR soldiers from Ghana. The tension thickened as it became clear that, instead of about 100 evacuees going to Kabuga, there were now several hundred and the lorries were packed, the canvas sides bulging. One lorry left for the interim-government zone. The hostility grew as our group was still loading; and those left behind in the Tutsi group were terrified because, as I learned later, they were now identifiable targets for Munyeshyaka's anger.

As the lorries finally rolled out, some 50 people were still left in the dusty compound. While we wondered aloud about their fate, the convoy, escorted by one UN armoured vehicle and some government soldiers (who left at the first roundabout) was attacked by *interahamwe*. Some of the evacuees were killed and wounded, ensuring that a second evacuation planned for the next day would not happen.

After about half an hour, we rolled into the battered little town of Kabuga. Hundreds of waiting relatives and friends gave us a tumultuous welcome, a small ray of hope in the fearsome misery.

A couple of months later, on a Sunday afternoon at the end of July, my friend Jean-Bosco Mukulira brought his 19-year-old sister Josepha to my house in Nairobi. She was one of the few members of his family he was able to extricate from the hellish

48

nightmare of Kigali. When she saw me, I thought for a moment she was going to faint.

"I saw you there that Friday with some other *bazungus* [a term for whites, meaning "those who replace you"], taking pictures and talking to the priest. The UN was taking some of us away but I could not get on the lorry. You remember, the convoy was shot at by the roundabout.

"That priest — you know him. You must have his picture. He was a killer. He organized to kill Tutsis right behind the church. He was very angry that you journalists took his picture. He told the *interahamwe* to attack you, and he killed some people that afternoon — ten of them I think."

I showed her the pictures of Odette and Fr Wenceslas. Her story, like many others, is one of sheer unrelenting terror and privation as she camped under a pew, locked in the stinking squalor of Holy Family Church, wondering day and night when the doors might open and the killers begin another massacre like the one in April when, Josepha said, the militias executed about a hundred Tutsi boys outside the church. "We could hear the machine guns and the boys screaming, but we could not see because we were lying on the floor. Since I was young, I was afraid I might be next."

Josepha has malaria and she is terribly thin. She talks to her brother and he translates. She wants to finish school and emigrate to Canada where another brother lives. She does not want to go back to Rwanda ever again.

"That priest — you know, at first we thought he was helping us, but then he became very angry at us Tutsis, and almost every day he sent some of us out to the killers. He pretended to you and the UN that he cared for all of us, but he wanted us dead. We were his hostages; he used us to keep the RPF from attacking." Her eyes are hollow, her voice often drops to a whisper. Her trauma will not end for a long time, if ever.

Just before the end of the year Jean-Bosco was married in Nairobi, and Josepha was one of the bridesmaids.

The big brown doors of Eglise Sainte Famille were open when I went to Kigali shortly after the war ended. Workers were repairing the huge bomb-hole in the roof. Damage from the bomb that had landed on Fr Wenceslas's bedroom roof — while he was away — had already been repaired. There was a new priest saying mass there, but he did not want to talk about the time during the war except to say that "some bad things happened here". There are differing reports about Fr Wenceslas. Some say he was killed in the final battle for Kigali, others that he is living in the camps in Zaire. Odette Nyirabagenzi's whereabouts at the time of writing are also unknown.

**Benaco**

Life in the camps was also one of bitter survival. Just getting to the camps was the first ordeal. Some 250,000 refugees jammed the road from the bridge that crosses the river between Rwanda and Tanzania, a tide of slowly moving people: women carrying the ubiquitous yellow plastic jerrycans; men with mattresses and bags of food; old people in wheelbarrows or stumping along with sticks; children, thousands of them alone without parents, most holding onto little pots and tins — an undulating stream of brightly coloured haze. The sun peeps over the horizon, already smudged with the wood-smoke of thousands of fires, the clogged roads taking the people, who emptied eastern Rwanda in 24 hours, to their sectors. Food trucks churn up the muddy roads until they are impassable, and still the people come, back and forth, seemingly aimless, looking for food, for water, for treatment of their many illnesses, for shelter, for a patch of brown grass to rest their weary bodies.

These are Hutus, told by their leaders who accompany them across the Rusumu Falls bridge that the advancing RPF will kill them all because they took part in the massacres. They put a small Tanzanian administrative centre, Ngara, on the world's television screens filled with flickering images of human suffering. The feeding and watering of 330,000 people crowded into 10 square kilometres at Benaco Camp in the arid bush of northwest Tanzania captured the world's attention. Then they are moved a little further on to another camp and then a third and a fourth as it becomes clear the Hutus are settling in for a long stay.

Peasants adapt quickly. Survival is the first priority in those early days. A big worry is the many children separated from their parents. Scarce wood has to be dragged from further and further away. Food lines are endless and chaotic. Women report being attacked by strange men. The search for water is unceasing. Shelter is non-existent, but soon little round huts emerge, later to be covered with blue and green plastic sheeting. It is an impossible situation, but the professionals from UNHCR, ICRC, Oxfam and other relief agencies move quickly to establish order and set up camps along the lines of the same sectors and communes the people are used to at home.

The Christian Council of Tanzania (CCT) and the Lutheran-operated Tanganyika Christian Refugee Service (TCRS), a part of Church World Action-Rwanda, move into the critical area of water supply. Preventing epidemics requires a minimum of ten litres of water a day per person, says UNHCR, and that will soon exhaust the already stretched water reserves. Bore-hole equipment and pumping systems, along with all the other necessities, are flown in through Mwanza airport and trucked 250 kilometres across impossible roads.

Thousands wait daily in the compounds for their food rations: 120 grammes of beans, 420 of maize, 50 of high protein soya blend, 25 grammes of oil and some salt, totalling, it says on the paper, 2000 calories — a lot more than the hospitable local Tanzanians are accustomed to, and a lot more than the refugees normally get at home. The world has been generous, once people got organized by the agencies, although in the first days people were on the verge of outright starvation. Mortality rates in Benaco never reached serious proportions, although people soon grumbled that there were not enough bananas or cassava, staples of the Rwandan diet. The church agencies handled transport from warehouses to distribution points. According to reports from CWA-R, the church agencies also brought in used clothing and blankets bought from Europe and the US, urgent because the Rwandese, accustomed to a balmier climate, suffered from respiratory ailments brought on by deluges of chilly rains.

CWA-R was born to help "to provide a comprehensive response to human needs" in response to this massive crisis, and soon launched its first appeal (the Pentecost Appeal) for US$9 million, which was ultimately over-subscribed by about US$2 million. Benaco was the first test of this joint operation of the Lutheran World Federation and World Council of Churches. Drawing on the long experience of TCRS, which has helped

Burundian refugees since 1962, its team of seven expatriates and almost a thousand local workers coped well with its mandate for water, transport and retrieving thousands of corpses from the Kagera River — and continues to. Although the flow of refugees has slowed and some have returned home, the camps remain full.

Tanzanian soldiers, at the border when the exodus began, confiscated thousands of machetes, suspecting that murderers among the refugees might try to continue the ethnic cleansing among the small number of Tutsis who also fled. Most were placed in a separate camp. However, Tanzania never had the resources to apprehend the killers who crossed over with the real refugees.

The killers quickly took over local control of the camps. Some even got work with relief agencies. Because UNHCR had organized the camps along Rwandan administrative lines, power was taken over by the same people who started the genocide inside the country. Violence and extortion rackets quickly became endemic, though not to the same extent as in Zaire later.

A widely publicized case was that of Jean-Baptiste Gatete. Mayor of Murambi and a known organizer of the genocide in Kibungo, he was arrested with some of his cohorts and was to have been expelled by the Tanzanian authorities in June. A riot in the camps, demanding their release, forced aid agencies temporarily to suspend operations when the UNHCR compound was threatened, roadblocks established and workers' lives at risk. Ultimately Gatete was removed from the camps and taken to Dar es Salaam. Authorities insist he will be returned to Rwanda when conditions for a fair trial exist there. Unfortunately, his is only the most obvious case; most of the killers are still at large in Benaco.

While most TCRS workers in the Tanzanian camps recognize the problem, they also insist the stories the refugees brought out of Rwanda paint a bloody picture of RPF assassinations in the areas bordering Tanzania and that as late as December bodies with fresh wounds were still being found in the river.

A UNHCR official reported in May that the majority of refugees who crossed in the first wave said they had seen people buried alive and tortured and slaughtered by out-of-control teenagers wearing unmarked uniforms and rubber boots. (Most RPF soldiers wore knee-high black rubber boots.) Some aid workers said they had heard shooting from across the river, which marks the border between Rwanda and Tanzania.

It is clear that the RPF did commit some atrocities, including the murder of three Roman Catholic bishops. But the evidence from refugees in Tanzania is mostly hearsay. *African Rights* quotes Jörg Zimmermann, a German pastor of the United Evangelical Mission who visited Ngara, as saying that "Benaco is no longer Tanzania. It is now part of MRND's Rwanda."

## Goma and Bukavu

The worst was yet to come. After its experience in Tanzania, one might have expected the international community to be prepared for further tragedy. Certainly there were warnings: Oxfam-UK constantly pleaded with the UNHCR to prepare for something that would make Benaco look like a Sunday School picnic. As the RPF began driving the FAR and militias out of their last bastion in the northwest part of the country from Gisenyi into Goma, about two million people streamed across the border to escape from what they had been told would be a slaughter by the rebels. The French kept warning that on August 31 they would withdraw from their self-proclaimed "safe zone" in southwest Rwanda, where another million or so were waiting to escape to Bukavu.

When the floodgates opened into the sleepy little town of Goma in mid-July, a solid human river 25 kilometres long poured across the border, overwhelming an unprepared UNHCR and turning the barren volcanic rock into a chaotic place of disease and death where ragged, destitute people choked the streets and died in their thousands of cholera and bloody dysentery.

"It is really the exodus of a nation. The whole country is bursting its borders and we cannot cope," said UNHCR spokesperson Panzos Moumtzis from the patio of Hotel du Grand Lac, a resort overlooking picturesque Lake Kivu. Beyond the bougainvillea-covered trellises was the most hideous scene imaginable: refugees living and dying on the volcanic fields of eastern Zaire in their millions. It was a staggering sight of unrelieved horror as Rwandese continuously shuffled past the razor wire separating the French army camp from the airport road.

Outside was such a tangle of abandoned corpses that soldiers simply scooped them up with front-end loaders and dumped them in mass graves carved out of the hard rock. There was no time or energy for even a prayer, let alone a thought about the dignity of human beings made in the image of God.

The refugees chopped down all the trees in Goma and tore up its grass for fires. Overnight the pleasant resort town of about 150,000 on the shores of a lovely lake became an indescribably filthy, sick city of 800,000 or more desperately poor people spread out to the edges of the lake as far as one could see through the stench and smoke. They tried to cook whatever they could find on the black rocks; and they were so ill that they defecated wherever they could, because there was no water and no latrines. Like so much having to do with Rwanda in 1994, it was beyond the capacity of the human mind to comprehend.

Despite the inhuman conditions, despite the RPF's bombing of Goma on the night of July 14, when 60 people were killed at the border-crossing, despite losing most of their meagre belongings to looting Zairean soldiers and police, from the beginning few of the refugees spoke of having any intention to return for two reasons: they feared RPF retaliation and they bore collective guilt for the massacres. By staying, they were fulfilling the plan of the self-appointed government all along.

From the outset, UNHCR and the relief agencies were completely overwhelmed. Everything — about 500 tons a day at first — had to be flown into the tiny, congested airport at Goma, where the French quickly took over the control tower. The first plane in was an LWF-chartered Hercules flown by South Africans, carrying supplies and two workers organized by CWA-R.

Local Zairean churches had almost no resources of their own. But they quickly opened up their buildings and compounds to the sick and dying refugees as a cholera outbreak, which killed some 50,000 people in those first days, swept through the disorganized camps. Pastors and volunteers worked until they dropped, bringing rehydration therapy and human concern to the mass of dying humanity. Every church and every compound was packed. People lay inside sanctuaries and on the ground, with unburied corpses nearby. Unprepared as anyone for such a tragedy, the local churches acted heroically and unselfishly, at great risk to their own health, as long as the horde of suffering people stayed in Goma and its environs. An Anglican archdeacon, tears in his eyes, said, "We do not even have time to pray for the dead or to bury them. The living must come first. To them, we must give moral and spiritual support and what food and medicines we can find."

Church people in Eastern Zaire had the impression of being ignored by the major agencies — the UN, ICRC, CARE, USAID, Médecins sans Frontières, even CWA-R. For some time Zairean church persons felt they were on their own, with no money to buy food and no way of obtaining the rehydration kits which was all that could save lives. Yet it was to their compounds and their volunteers that the first waves of refugees had to turn; and without them and their open-hearted support, many more refugees would have died.

"We are perplexed that none of the church agencies has even tried to contact us, except World Vision. All around us is death, death, death. We are living in a sea of bodies. All day and night you can hear the whimpering of children. We are doing our best," said Archdeacon Katanda Masimango, whose Anglican parish was crammed with dead and dying people.

Pastor Palukus Musuvagho, the president of the Goma branch of the Church of Christ in Zaire (ECZ), acknowledged that the tragedy was beyond the churches' capacity. "Every Christian family I know, including all the pastors, have opened their homes and compounds. I have 40 people living in my own house.

"It is too much. We don't know what to do and we cannot get any help from our partners. We are already worn down, and even our volunteers are short of food. It seems CWA-R doesn't recognize local churches as partners. They would rather work with the UN."

The criticism, although genuinely felt, was unfair. Goma was in utter chaos. The airport was impossible, transport was in short supply and communications were hopeless, since Zaire has no functioning telephone system. The first two CWA-R staff to arrive, Patricia Nickson and John Parker, did not even have a vehicle when they were interviewed on July 20. Within a few days, however, some rudimentary co-ordination was in place. CWA-R supplies were being fed into the UN pipeline, pastors and volunteers were getting cholera-treatment kits and some semblance of support was being given the emaciated and terribly ill refugees.

It was only a matter of time before other waves of refugees fled south of Goma from the French zone into Bukavu at the opposite end of Lake Kivu. Efforts to persuade the refugees to return home — or later to stay in the "safe zone" once the French had left — failed, even though UNAMIR-II promised to "guarantee" their safety. They believed the propaganda that the Tutsi-dominated RPF would exterminate them. Radio Mille Collines, now on wheels, pumped out stories of massacres, although few could be confirmed by the UN. Statements by the new government in Kigali that it planned to put 30,000 people on trial within a month did little to encourage return. Most of all, the people were cowed by the intimidation and terrorism practised by the former government and its army and militias, whose presence was pervasive. Those who tried to return to Rwanda were beaten, tortured or killed — or simply disappeared — while the former army and militias rendered the camps unsafe, leaving aid workers in fear and allowing the extremists to control food distribution. By the end of 1994, the five-month-old government had done little to persuade the refugees to return home, and stories of reprisal killings continued to drift across the border.

Among the fugitives in those weeks following the two main exoduses — first into Goma, then, after the French pulled out, to the area around Bukavu — were some 40,000 defeated but well-organized troops. They swaggered through the camps, looting food with impunity from sick and malnourished refugees. Half-hearted attempts by Zairean troops to disarm them filtered out some of the heavier weapons, but in the confusion many soldiers and officers managed to keep their guns, although they were out of ammunition.

Unlike the victorious RPF soldiers, the Hutu fighters are paid and well-fed. By late 1994, the army had fairly well regrouped in special camps preparing intensively to restart the war. In training bases north of Bukavu, they are said to be recruiting thousands of teenagers from the refugee camps and bringing the regular and professional militias back into fighting trim, ready to wage guerilla and conventional war to force the Kigali government into a power-sharing arrangement with the extremists, something Vice President Kagame has vowed will never happen, even if it means fighting another war.

Aid workers know of all this activity but are powerless, it seems, to do anything about it. Grandiose plans for a UN military force to police the camps have fallen through due to a lack of funds and commitment.

"We saved the lives of those who did the massacres, then we fed them and now we have essentially turned the camps over to them while they prepare for another war and another massive outflow of refugees and perhaps even another genocide," said one ICRC representative at Christmas. The sub-region is awash with weapons. The old government has strong links with the Zairean authorities, especially President Mobutu, and there seems to be no shortage of money for retraining and re-equipping the army.

If Benaco was a reproach to the international community, with its inability to look beyond emergencies, Goma was — and is — an abject failure. Long gone from the screens of CNN, Rwanda seems also to have disappeared from the foreign policy of Northern countries, where the attention of the voters has long since been diverted back to the bloody ethnic battles of Eastern Europe and Russia. Many agencies have already withdrawn, looking for more lucrative places to raise funds. CWA-R launched an Advent Appeal in November for US$17 million, but some European fund-raising experts doubted that more than a third of this could be raised, although the WCC and LWF insist that they are in solidarity with Rwanda and neighbouring countries for the long haul.

With the stomach-churning pictures gone and the UN network mired in indecision, churches and humanitarian agencies fear another outbreak of war which could engulf the entire region around the lakes, drawing into the crisis countries which have hitherto been less affected. Chipenda fears that Burundi, lurching from crisis to crisis, may be further embroiled in similar violence and he expresses "grave anxiety" about the long-term future.

"The infrastructure of Rwanda remains largely destroyed. The country has neither the means nor the resources to resume administrative and economic activity. Humanitarian aid is entirely in the hands of international agencies, but they cannot solve the problems and, indeed, unintentionally exacerbate them," he said early in 1995. "The solution lies with restoration of government institutions and services and a rule of law supported and sanctioned by the international community but in the control of Rwandese."

The AACC general secretary, who has made many pastoral visits to Rwanda and neighbouring countries, also points to the destabilizing situation of long-term refugees now under the control of the former authorities in Rwanda.

## To save the children

About one-third of those killed in Rwanda's genocide — somewhere between 250,000 and 300,000 — were children; and almost all of those who survived are in various stages of emotional and physical trauma.

Graca Machel, widow of Mozambique's late president Samora Machel and head of a special UN commission on the impact of war on children, has had many years of experience in helping youngsters recover from the devastation of war, especially in her own country. Visiting orphanages and groups of children scattered about Rwanda and in refugee camps was, she said, the most "hellish" experience of her career. She says their experiences will scar most of them for life.

Machel says large-scale trauma programmes are needed but doubts, on the basis of her experiences in Mozambique, that much will be done due to a shortage of resources and also cultural differences. "Perhaps now the most effective and least costly thing that can be done is to make sure they are shown a great deal of love and security. They should remain in their own environment with people they can trust." Machel opposes large-scale adoptions by foreigners.

They have been pulled from heaps of stinking corpses or found wandering alone, aimlessly and helplessly, through the deserted countryside. They sit in small groups of tents beside the road, staring blankly as volunteers try to feed and nurse them back to health, their tiny emaciated bodies shuddering with dysentery and diarrhoea.

In some ways these are the fortunate ones: they are still alive. Inside Rwanda during the genocide, children's bodies were often seen sprawled among the corpses of adults, many clutched tightly by their mothers as if to protect them to the end from being beaten, shot or hacked to death. Like the rest of the genocide, the killing of children, especially Tutsi boys, was not accidental. Many eyewitnesses reported militias deliberately killing pregnant women, babies and young children because they were the future Tutsi generation. A story repeated often was "Remember, Kagame was only two when he left for Uganda." Rwanda's new vice-president left for exile in 1959 with his parents, grew up and returned at the head of the victorious army.

Children also killed other children, forced or encouraged by adults. UNICEF recently completed a study which says 40 percent of the children they interviewed in late August had witnessed killings by children under 15 and even younger. More than half of the survivors had seen family members being killed and most had seen other people killed.

"The children are haunted by the sights, smells and sounds of people dying. They are struggling with and haunted by the memories of what they experienced," the report states.

At the ICRC hospital in Kigali in mid-May there were two tents at the back of the complex, a former school located near the front-lines in FAR territory, wedged between a brick wall and a hill for safety from the shelling. More than 50 little children were being treated there for all sorts of horrible wounds. One little boy's head and much of his tiny body was covered in bandages from shrapnel wounds. He couldn't speak. Another child sat smiling at some inner thing he could not express; both his ears had been chopped off. A girl, perhaps five, sang a little song, seemingly ignoring the stump of her arm, amputated above the elbow. A boy had no foot.

A volunteer doctor from California said the footless boy told him he and some friends were playing on a Kigali street — he did not know where his parents were — when killers came along and chopped off one boy's foot and another boy's hand.

Many of the children in the tent were on stretchers, most of them either orphaned or unaware of where their parents were. Some had been badly beaten. Rwandan Red Cross workers told of finding a seven-year-old girl lying inert across a tree trunk, brutally raped.

Shelling also took its toll. The day I visited the hospital a baby had just been brought in, streaming blood, along with several other children with shrapnel wounds, all screaming in pain and fear. A Dutch nurse said this was an almost daily occurrence.

At an SOS Children's Village near Byumba, in early June, volunteer teachers helped to ease the trauma of some 700 children hidden from the still-active *interahamwe*. Many were swathed in bandages from machete cuts. Their ages ranged from eight months to 14 years. Many had seen their parents killed.

Rose Kayitesi is a teacher in Burundi who came as a volunteer to help orphan children being cared for by the RPF in a former luxury hotel owned by President Habyarimana's brother-in-law in a recently liberated zone not far from the Uganda border.

"They have all the signs of emotionally damaged children," she told me. "They have terrible nightmares, they wet their beds, they can't sleep, many can't talk. Their trauma is intense."

Most of the children were still thin and weak, many had not eaten for days; others still could not eat. All had nutritional problems. Five, Rose Kayitesi said, were "completely insane". She said it was too soon to say if they were orphans. No one knows where their parents are, except those who saw them killed.

Emmanuel Sibomana from Nyanza is 12. He stands almost at attention, his head covered in bandages, in a kitchen where he has been helping to cook maize porridge. He tells his story in a halting stutter, his eyelids blinking rapidly, and Rose Kayitesi's arm about his thin shoulders.

> They came to my grandmother's house where my mother and sister and I were staying after my father was killed in a school where he was hiding. First they shot my grandmother, but she didn't die right away, then they killed my sister and cut me on the head. My mother ran away to get help and then she came back but they were

chasing her and she was cut on her legs. Then they set the [kerosene] stove on fire and the house began to burn. My grandmother, although she was badly hurt, helped me get away but my mother died in the fire. We hid in the burned-out kitchen of the house but my grandmother died and I was left alone. I was very weak. I stayed alone for a long time and then the RPF came along and found me and brought me to a clinic and I got better and now I can help the cooks. I was saved by God.

All over Rwanda one hears similar stories of the most appalling cruelty to children. Some mothers killed their children or threw them into rivers rather than allow them to be clubbed or beaten to death. One mother told me how she ran across a field, chased by militias, carrying her baby on her back in the African way. They clubbed the baby to a pulp, but for reasons she does not know, she was allowed to live.

The rehabilitation of orphans and children who cannot find their parents is an enormous task far beyond the resources of the government and international NGOs. After the war, an AACC delegation visited orphanages in several parts of the country. Most of the children showed signs of their ordeals, although their physical condition was improving and some were even going to school. But their emotional state was often heart-rending, as little ones clutched at the visitors' legs and hands and would not let go, many screaming when they were gently detached. Others sat with arms wrapped around legs or curled in little balls of misery. Some just stared; some rocked back and forth for hours; some picked anxiously at sores and scabs from old wounds. They had seen more death in their few years than most of us could manage in a lifetime.

Experts say their healing will require years of work. Many may never recover. Child psychologists from UNICEF worry that an entire generation of deeply disturbed youngsters will grow up with little understanding of the emotional and physical violence done to them, and will themselves become anti-social and violent as they grow older, forcing the ills of the past on an already emotionally overwrought society. Churches, in whose buildings so many children were brutalized, have a special responsibility for the healing of the innocents.

In the refugee camps too, especially in Zaire, the tiny ones were the first victims of disease and starvation. Weakened by the ordeal of running, they fell prey to the first ravages of cholera and dysentery. Some of the most wrenching sights during those early days in Goma were piles of corpses by the roadside, wrapped in mats. On the top were the tiny bundles, less than a metre long, the initial victims of the exodus. Young boys and girls staggered along the roadsides amid the stench of excrement and sickness and decomposing bodies, carrying their dying little brothers or sisters.

In the church compounds of Goma, parents sat, weak and glassy-eyed from the epidemics which swept like a forest fire through the city, holding an emaciated little body or watching hollow-eyed as a child died and they could do nothing. In a Baptist churchyard, a mother and a young boy, perhaps four or five, lay to one side of a veranda on the unrelenting volcanic rock, covered with a filthy cloth, facing one another. The mother was shockingly thin and weak. Her son stared into her face. She tried to lift one hand, perhaps to comfort him, a last act of love. She could barely move. Soon they would become yet another statistic as the health workers moved on to those who still had strength to survive.

Even more difficult to face were those who had gotten lost during the long trek through the hills and could not find their families. Too young or sick or traumatized to talk, they knew only that they were abandoned. In the first days of the Goma tragedy, church workers gently gathered those they found wandering alone or loosely attached to another group and brought them to small camps, hoping that in a few days parents would come looking. At one camp there were at least ten thousand. Many still do not know where their mothers and fathers are, or if they are alive at all.

These assaults on children are one of the worst legacies of the genocide. In addition to the slaughter and the wounding in body and spirit, there is the enormous job of reunification in a country where almost all records have been destroyed or lost in the looting sprees that accompanied the massacres. UNICEF and ICRC and other agencies with expertise in reuniting families will try to find parents or relatives, but it is a colossal job and, in the end, thousands will have no immediate family to care for them and give them the love which they deserve and which they will need if they are to be healed.

Not far from Rwanda's border with Zaire, relief workers found a little child, perhaps two or three, wailing in terror as he tried to awaken his dead mother. "I came closer. His screams grew with his fear of a white person. I gained his trust slowly, slowly and then he just clung to me like glue," said Pat Nickson of CWA-R.

* * *

Many people died in Rwanda. Many others survived with an extraordinary tenacity and will to live despite a tragedy which no words can describe. That tenacity and human spirit are all that remains for the vast majority of the living. The international community, including the African community and the community of God's people, *must* do what is right: make certain that this will to live is honoured and not further wasted by ensuring that justice, peace and reconciliation follow hard on the heels of humanitarian aid.

# 5. The Church: Problems and Promises

> You who are our pastors, how many times have you visited the people who are sick and suffering? Do you know where they live, the condition of their houses, what they eat, the things they are most in need of? Can you identify with their problems, the scale of these problems? Why do you make friends only with the well-off people, the oppressors of the workers?
>
> Your very affluent style of life (luxury cars, fashionable clothes, expensive houses) increases the gap between you and us ordinary people, and this adds to our lack of confidence in you. The Christians feel abandoned, whereas you and your priests ought to be the voice of the voiceless, the outcasts, and serve the common folks.
>
> You have to teach the Christians about democracy, non-violence and human rights, and help them live these values in their family and places of work. Religious leaders clearly ought to be the first ones to live and practise them.

These words are taken from an open letter addressed by the Rwanda Association of Christian Workers to the first African synod of Roman Catholic bishops.

Pope John Paul II opened this special synod in Rome on April 10, just four days after Habyarimana's plane was shot down. Already priests and religious sisters had been killed in their scores. The Christus Centre massacre had received wide media coverage. The nine Rwandese bishops were unable to join the other 315 bishops at the pontifical high mass in St Peter's Basilica, where drums and African songs throbbed in a colourful eucharistic liturgy, but the theme of the synod was heavy with symbolism for them: "You shall be my witnesses" (Acts 1:8).

## Voices of warning and appeal

The pope's homily had extraordinarily strong words about Rwanda:

> I wish to recall in particular the people and the church of Rwanda who these days are being tried by an overwhelming tragedy. With you bishops here present I am sharing this suffering caused by the new catastrophic wave of violence and death which is making blood flow even from priests, religious sisters and religion teachers, innocent victims of an absurd hatred.
>
> I raise my voice to tell all of you: Stop these acts of violence. Stop these fratricidal massacres.

64

In Rwanda, only a few church leaders or their followers listened to the pope's cry of suffering for the people of this country which he had visited four years earlier. Little did he know that before the synod ended a month later, hundreds of thousands, including three of his bishops and half their priests, would be victims. The Catholic Church as an institution would be decimated, as would its Protestant counterparts.

One of the synod's first acts was to approve an urgent plea to the army, the militias, the RPF and everyone connected with the killings to "lay down their arms and stop the atrocities and the killing. *All* the people of Rwanda are entitled to life — something that every African loves and values."

Even before John Paul spoke out, José Chipenda — who also made an eloquent and early intervention at the synod — had warned on April 7 of the dangers of an impending genocide and called for an immediate end to the killings. His statement alerted northern partner churches, AACC member churches and national Christian councils in Africa of the grave dangers ahead. He also urged a redoubling of UNAMIR's vigilance in protecting civilians. It was painful to be in the AACC headquarters as first the UN withdrew, then the overseas partners responded half-heartedly, if at all.

Chipenda's first statement was the beginning of a critical process of information-sharing and action-oriented statements in order to make available all possible communications about the tragic events and to appeal to the worldwide ecumenical movement to use its influence to end the horror. By the end of 1994 the AACC had issued some 30 special informational updates on the situation, organized a worldwide day of prayer (July 31) and worked tirelessly to bring about reconciliation. With insufficient budget for a tragedy of such proportions, the AACC ran up a serious deficit in its efforts to help Rwanda in its travail and to keep the moral issues before the world church. Sadly, it took some weeks and a widely televised refugee crisis of monumental proportions to galvanize churches into action. "It did too little, too late," Chipenda later said at a CWA-R meeting in Geneva.

In letters to Boutros-Ghali and Salim Salim on May 4, three weeks after the genocide began, Chipenda expressed his agony and frustration:

The eyes of Africa today are filled with tears. On the one hand, we weep with joy at the wonderful display of democracy and peace in South Africa. But, on the other hand, my dear African brothers, we are overwhelmed with anguish at the massacres and senseless violence in Rwanda, where we believe suffering on a magnitude the world has seldom seen is taking place in a situation where African countries and the international community appear both uncaring and impotent.

## A silent and compromised church

Inside Rwanda, the church leadership, both Catholic and Protestant, was silent, compromised and paralyzed, except for a few individuals who risked and often lost their lives to protect and minister to their people.

More than 90 percent of Rwanda's people were baptized Christians (65 percent Catholic, 20 percent Protestant or Anglican, about 5 percent Adventist). There were a small number of Muslims — some of whom were also massacred — and animists.

Except for the government itself, the Roman Catholic Church was the most influential and powerful institution in Rwanda. The Protestant churches, though numerically much smaller, had a disproportionate degree of influence right up to the office of the president. Church leaders, who received patronage and lavish gifts from the ruling party, too often remained silent in the face of injustice, unwilling to exert the authority of their positions in the moral vacuum within Rwandan society in Habyarimana's last years. Their statements during the genocide and in the chaos that followed were inadequate and insignificant, often sounding as if they had been written by a public relations person for the interim government. For this silent acquiescence and lack of courage, the churches as institutions paid dearly. They will continue to live under a cloud of suspicion for years to come. Meanwhile, the church internationally was unable or unwilling to provide anything like the unquestioning support and solidarity it gave for more than 25 years to the victims of apartheid in South Africa.

Now the churches in Rwanda, along with the rest of the country, must enter a painful period of mourning and self-reflection before the healing which will allow for peace and reconciliation can happen. Attempts to short-circuit this process by denying what happened and moving directly into reconstruction and rehabilitation could lead to repeating the problems of the past.

After a visit to Rwanda, Zaire and Burundi late in 1994, seven AMECEA bishops expressed solidarity with their sisters and brothers but cautioned that grieving and mourning are God's way of healing. It cannot be painless, it cannot be cheap, it cannot be replaced by mindless activism.

A member of the Missionaries of Africa order (formerly known as the White Fathers), which came to Rwanda a hundred years ago, says:

> We are very worried that people are deliberately, or as a survival mechanism, bypassing their mourning. We participated in several liturgies which, to be frank, were as if nothing had happened. They were liturgies which we used ten years ago when I was a missionary in Rwanda. There was no acknowledgment that anything bad had happened. It is very serious. People must not suppress their grief or it will emerge in negative ways later on.

For these very reasons, Chipenda keeps insisting to the Rwanda churches, his colleagues at AACC and the partners in CWA-R that the peace and reconciliation process will need support for years. He told a November meeting in Nairobi which brought together Catholic, Protestant and evangelical church leaders with Rwandese exiles:

> It is a process that begins with sorrow and grief, repentance, forgiveness, justice, reconciliation and peace. To make it a six-month or year-long project, for example, starting with workshops and seminars, is futile. We cannot set it up this way; it will be a long, slow process, which will require patience and solidarity from the rest of Africa and overseas. But ultimately it is the people of God and their leaders inside Rwanda who must be healed and reconciled. That is a reality which must be accepted.

It was clear during these and other meetings with church leaders inside Rwanda and those in the camps of Zaire and Tanzania who will not go home that the depths of the trauma have not been understood, nor have most people begun to purge themselves of the hatred which encouraged the genocide and allowed it to reach such apocalyptic proportions.

More than two-thirds of Rwanda's Catholic priests are either dead or in exile. At the end of 1994, only two of the nine bishops were in the country. Three had been killed, two were ill and two in exile. The figures for Protestant leaders are similar. Only three of eleven Anglican bishops were inside the country. Most church buildings have been destroyed or looted and were the sites of widespread and horrific massacres.

Mainline Protestant churches, as well as the Roman Catholic leadership, were perceived as being close to the hard-line Hutu extremist ideology. But even the third-largest religious grouping, the Seventh-day Adventists, who were largely apolitical, reported that the killings were as bad in their areas as anywhere else.

"People seem to have lost their sense of the sacred. It must be recovered patiently and with courage to rebuild trust and mutual acceptance. Moving from despair to hope, from disinformation to the truth, from revenge to forgiveness, we must deal with why this all happened," the AMECEA bishops said in a final statement when they left Rwanda at the end of November.

AACC and Catholic leaders both urged, in separate long meetings with the president and prime minister, that the new government create conditions conducive to the return of the refugees, especially by ending revenge killings and disappearances by unruly teenage soldiers and summary arrests without specific charges.

The genocide shook the very foundations of all the churches: none remained without blood on its hands. Not only were hundreds of religious workers killed but hundreds of thousands of faithful parishioners and members were slaughtered in churches which they had been taught to believe were safe sanctuaries and havens from violence. Many believe they were betrayed by their leaders.

It was not just Josephine in Ntarama who told me she would never enter the church of her youth again. While many people are still devout and wish to live the Christian life, they see the old churches more as grave-sites than places of worship and peace. They yearn for and are demanding a church that is rebuilt and, before it is, a willingness on the part of some of the leaders to repent and face their people — perhaps even justice before a war crimes tribunal. This new church, which some call the "surviving church" or the "repentant church", will come from the bottom and the fringes, and will select its own leaders.

It is a tragic irony that the year of massacres was the centenary of the coming to Rwanda of Christian missionaries, many of whose successors now express bitterness and anger at their leaders, especially towards Roman Catholic Archbishop Vincent Nsengiyumva and Anglican Archbishop Augustin Nshamihigo. The former was killed with two other bishops and 13 priests by RPF soldiers who were supposed to be guarding them; the latter was still in Goma at the time of writing, keeping in close touch with the former government.

A Hutu priest in Kigali says the failure of the church to provide moral leadership is inexplicable. The position of the bishops in Rwandese society should have been enormously important. They knew of the impending disaster long before the killings were unleashed. Church pulpits could have provided an opportunity for almost the entire population to hear a strong message that could have prevented the genocide. Instead the leaders remained silent.

Fr Jean-Baptiste Rugengamanzi, acting administrator of Kigali's Roman Catholic archdiocese, says that "at the level of faith, this is horrible. Ours is a church which celebrates 100 years of Christianity. I can't explain it. The tragedy is that the horror of the massacres surpassed the limits of people's faith."

The churches were as divided as the country. Many accounts can be told of heroism in standing up to the killers, but the leadership had been co-opted. Nsengiyumva, for example, was a key member and social affairs chair of the Central Committee of the MRND for 14 years until he was urged by the Vatican to step down from that post in 1990. He was also Mme Habyarimana's personal confessor.

## A few small voices

Not until weeks after the pope demanded an end to the killings in his synodical address did the church leaders issue any serious public statement. By then many Catholic leaders and priests had fled Kigali for the relative safety of Kabgayi, which was also closer to the Gitarama-based interim government. On May 13, Protestant leaders and four Catholic bishops produced a conciliatory document which apportioned blame equally to the RPF and "the Rwandese government" and called on both to "stop the massacres".

Nshamihigo did not endorse even this mild statement, although four other Anglican bishops did, along with the president of the Presbyterian Church, Michel Twagirayesu, a member of the Central Committee of the WCC and former vice-president of the AACC, and the legal representatives of the Methodist, Free Methodist, Baptist and Pentecostal churches.

The document never mentioned genocide and refrained from naming the organizers of the evil. In essence it expressed "condolences" to the victims; called for an end to massacres by both sides; offered to mediate between the two sides to set up a new "transitional" government; requested a "neutral military force" from the UN; called for help from "friendly" governments to look for a "negotiated" solution; "disapproved" of acts of desecration and destruction of "sacred places" and the killing of "apostolic workers"; and "requested" all Christians to "refuse" participation in massacres and "acts of pillaging and vandalism" and instead to pray for peace.

In contrast to the pope's demands for an end to killings and "absurd hatred" and Chipenda's equally strong statement of April 7, Rwanda's church leaders were cautious to the point of missing the prophetic and pastoral calling rooted in biblical and church imperatives to speak justice in all seasons.

Now, as one visits church buildings in Rwanda, many of them still containing bloodstains and bleached bones, their walls and roofs bomb-damaged and their sanctuaries pock-marked with bullet holes and pitted from fragmentation grenades, one can begin to understand how the church mirrored society instead of standing against evil and for justice. While there were wonderful acts of heroism, sacrifice and even martyrdom, many priests and pastors ran away from their people, remained inactive or committed heinous acts of betrayal and murder, whether forced at gunpoint or voluntarily.

Many of these fled to Tanzania and Zaire, some still loyal to the ousted government, the defeated army and the vicious militias, where they found the safety denied to their parishioners in their churches. Others who remained behind during the genocide and war and saved thousands of lives must now struggle with the pain of losing their closest family members, the sense of failure as they saw members of their own congregations killing one another, the destruction of sacred buildings and holy places and the betrayal of many of their leaders.

Some simply cannot forgive and have turned away from the structured church to a faith that is no longer connected to the past. Others try to preach forgiveness and, even more difficult, to practise it.

"I will try to ask God to teach me how to forgive," says Fr Nicodeme Nayigiziki, a Tutsi priest at the Roman Catholic Cathedral of St Michel, who hid in Kigali all through the war with some of his parishioners and helped to hide many Hutus sought by the death squads:

> There is much work to be done in the church. People have told me they will not enter churches in which people were killed. This makes me sad because many people have been killed in churches. The church was far too close to the government. Perhaps it should have separated itself from partisan politics. There were many signs of what was happening but we did nothing. I hope we will learn about the signs of the times. In the future there will probably be fewer Catholics, but those who come through this ordeal will have a stronger faith.

One of the many martyrs of Rwanda's terror was Nayigiziki's counterpart, the dean of the Anglican Cathedral Church of St Etienne, Canon Alphonse Karuhije, also a Tutsi, who is credited with saving many lives.

Early in the war he sent his wife and children to relatives in Tanzania for safety, but he would not desert his flock even after his bishop fled. As the killings became more intense and war came closer to St Etienne's, the cathedral compound was severely damaged, but the dean continued trying to help. By day, he was forced often to hide in one of the two square towers of his cathedral because the *interahamwe* were always on the prowl, looking for people they should kill.

Then one day in early June his hiding place was invaded. He was hacked to pieces in what must have been a long and horrible ordeal.

On August 25 St Etienne's held its first service after the war ended. Standing on the small balcony between the two towers, taking pictures of the large congregation of ecumenical worshippers close to the site of his martyrdom, was a poignant moment for me: I had learned just a few minutes earlier that Canon Karuhije had been turned in to the killers by a fellow priest.

The eucharistic celebration that day was one of pain and joy. There were no phones in those early days after the war, no way except word of mouth to notify the community that there would be a service. The cathedral roof was a tracery of bullet holes. The sanctuary walls were gouged with holes made by mortars, but the huge dove of peace painted over the altar was somehow unscarred. The poor and the weak and the frightened and the lonely, the widows and the small ones without parents began arriving, more than 500 of them. Greetings were deeply moving as one person after another discovered relatives and friends they did not know had survived. They were thin and hungry and sick, their houses destroyed or looted, their experiences haunting, their hopes uncertain, but did they sing and pray and share the sacrament placed in their trembling hands by priests and ministers from many denominations and places. It was the Church of the Survivors, still unsure of its future but for those few hours at least a community once again.

## A meeting in Kigali

Three weeks earlier, when the stench of death still hung over the empty green hills and when people were still crawling out from under the debris of their lives and homes, a small delegation from CWA-R flew into Kigali, among other things to meet with pastors who had survived the genocide. The meeting was held in a hall that was part of a Presbyterian church. Most of the roof had been blown off and the nave was littered with pieces of cement and all the other detritus of war and neglect.

About 20 people were present at the meeting, chaired by Pastor Naasson Hitimana, a former president of the Presbyterian Church in Rwanda. Their clothes were fairly ragged; they had lost everything, including many family members. Their homes had been looted, as had their church and personal bank accounts. They had no money and very little food or medicine. They were exhausted, and they said they were in dire need of spiritual care.

It began like many church meetings. Everyone sat in a squared circle, carefully shaking hands, greeting the four visitors from the LWF, WCC and AACC and introducing themselves. But then it became like no other church meeting I had ever attended.

There were four pastors, the widows of two pastors killed in the massacres, three elders, a deacon and an evangelist. Each was a survivor. Each had a painful story. All were there to support the others and to begin rebuilding their church only days after the new government was appointed.

As churches usually do, they had formed a committee, the Presbyterian Committee for Rehabilitation, which quickly became known as the Surviving Church and then, when more people came home, the Repentant Church. They had drafted a document, painfully pecked out in French on a typewriter that had somehow escaped the looters, called *SOS pour les Presbytériens rescapés du génocide au Rwanda* ("SOS for Presbyterian survivors of the Rwanda genocide").

It is important to understand their ordeal and how they presented it to the CWA-R visitors. They began by thanking God for sparing their lives from the genocide — unlike many church leaders they had no difficulty using that term. Then came a simple, basic recounting of what had happened and whom they knew as of July 28 to have been killed. There were 17 family names, almost every one accompanied by the words *"avec sa famille"* or *"et toute sa famille"* ("with his family" or "and all his family"). It was a litany of death, and this was only the first accounting.

> We realized that our church had lost many of its members... Every Tutsi and some Hutus who did not want to co-operate with the militias had to be killed. Nobody was allowed to hide another, but the Hutus were incited to take machetes and kill their neighbours, friends and relatives from the Tutsi ethnic group.
>
> They went on to kill even the elderly over 80 years old and pregnant women who were believed to have a Tutsi husband, killing the mother or killing the baby upon delivery. Those who managed to escape had been hiding for two months or more in the bush, in sewers, in some Catholic parishes and in hotels.

The language was sparse, the more horrifying in its simplicity.

We do not know the fate of most of our flock. The number of orphans and widows and widowers is high. The churches and houses have been destroyed or looted. Spiritual care is very scarce because church personnel have been murdered or run to Zaire and Tanzania.

Church salaries have not been paid for April, May, June or July...

We need help.

There were no angry recriminations or accusations, simply statements of fact. Some questions, though.

Hitimana, a wise and gentle man with a kind smile, said the African and world churches should have come sooner to help. "You took too long." A colleague agreed: "The international community watched and did not help us. Neither did the churches, whom we hoped would condemn the atrocities, because we are and have been loyal members of the WCC and the AACC."

They wondered aloud why Michel Twagirayesu, whom they knew was in the refugee camps at Bukavu, had not returned. "We have sent word that it is safe to come back. People who ran away to Bukavu and Goma and Ngara are getting help, but no help has come here," said Hitimana.

There was lengthy analysis of the causes of the genocide. They examined their own role and found it wanting. Elder Justin Hakizimana looked tired and pained:

The church went hand-in-hand with the politics of Habyarimana. We did not condemn what was going on because we were corrupted. None of our churches, especially the Catholics, has condemned the massacres. That is why all the church leaders have fled, because they believe they may be in trouble with their people. They must return as individuals, not as leaders and then we will judge them and see if they are fit to be leaders. If not, they must resign.

They emphasized that the church and the government had become too close, so close that the leaders could not criticize the corruption or give up their status and their gifts — cars, televisions, guaranteed places in the school system for children and relatives. "It is time the church and the government got a divorce," said Deacon Ananie Twagirimana.

Words like "shame" and "embarrassment" and "sadness" began to emerge as they groped for explanations of the churches' failure. In the words of Pastor Aaron Mugemera, "the church didn't change people; instead, the church was changed and became weak. People joined extremist political parties and went to political meetings on Sunday instead of going to church. Then when the massacres began, people became worse than animals because our message had become so superficial."

Jesse Mugambi, representing the AACC, told them that the church as an institution could be destroyed, but "the church as the people of God can never be destroyed. Do not give up hope."

At this meeting, and at a second with Chipenda three weeks later, some of the pastors made a comparison with the Confessing Church in Nazi Germany. In Rwanda, they said, there were two churches and many denominations — the official church, almost all of whose leaders were close to government, and another church which is now the Surviving Church. Some of these pastors stood firm and refused to accept the killings. They spoke out, and they matched their words with actions by hiding people in their houses at great risk. One pastor said:

> I was hiding people in Kigali. I never left. They were in my ceiling and the militias came. I showed them my children and asked if the children were enemies, and they were ashamed and went away. The leader of the militia group who surrounded my house that day was a member of my congregation. When he went away, I decided to leave because it was not safe, but I took all the people hiding in my house with me and today they are still alive.

The pastors seemed determined that the church of the future should transcend denominationalism. "Unity is more important than anything," said Mugemera. "How can we talk to our people about reconciliation when we are divided? I have seen many terrible things in Rwanda — dogs eating the bodies of people I knew — and we have lost all our credibility because of the bad actions of our leaders. It is painful and embarrassing to have people ask for help when we cannot even help ourselves. The church is in shame."

Mugemera is alone. His entire family, six children and his spouse, was butchered by militias before his eyes. He was in hiding when *interahamwe* burst into the house where they had fled for safety. As he watched, unable to do anything, the seven were hacked to death. To add to his pain, the killers were members of his congregation, some of whom he had baptized. His sad eyes reflect his loneliness and pain.

> Why did the message of the gospel not reach the people who were baptized? What did we lose? We lost our lives. We lost our credibility. We are ashamed. We are weak. But, most of all, we lost our prophetic mission. We could not go to the President and tell him the truth because we became sycophants to the authorities.
>
> We have had killings here since 1959. No one condemned them. During the First Republic, they killed slowly, slowly, but no one from the churches spoke out. No one spoke on behalf of those killed. During the Second Republic there were more killings and more people were tortured and raped and disappeared; and we did not speak out because we were afraid, and because we were comfortable.
>
> Now there has to be a new start, a new way. We must accept that Jesus' mission to us to preach the gospel means that we must be ready to protect the sheep, the flock — even if it means we must risk our lives — to lay down our lives for our sisters and brothers. The Bible does not know Hutu and Tutsi, neither should we.

The church in Rwanda is in an agony at least as painful as the nation's. While Christians continue to meet, seeking solace and sustenance from lay leaders and pastors, their leaders languish in Nairobi or in the refugee camps, unwilling to return for fear of their safety. They claim that the arrest of some 7000 people by the RPF on flimsy evidence makes their return impossible. Inside the country, the churches which have traditionally had a more collegial structure seem more able to recover their battered mission than those with strong hierarchies whose leaders are absent.

The call for guidance and support from the Protestant Council of Rwanda (CPR) is strong. Its offices and compound were severely damaged during the war and the contents looted extensively. During a CWA-R visit, observers saw files and computer discs scattered across the compound in the midst of piles of clothing, smashed furniture, live ammunition, shell casings and a burned-out vehicle. Windows and security bars were broken and all items of value stolen.

Emmanuel Nkusi, the council's general secretary, has accompanied several church delegations to Rwanda but has so far declined to return, preferring to stay in Nairobi with his family because he is convinced the new government cannot assure his safety if he returns. He cites examples of people who have disappeared and the claims of exiled church leaders that it is unsafe until a broad-based government is in place and refugees can return.

## Understanding the churches' failure

Theories and after-the-fact analysis about the churches' failures abound. It will be a long time before a new church arises from the ashes of the old. Journalists have concentrated on the church compound slaughters without questioning why so many deaths occurred in places normally considered sacred or why there was such desecration by people who would normally regard symbols of faith with almost superstitious reverence.

Some Rwandese church people attribute the desecrations to a deliberate strategy by the extremists to destroy any alternatives to their ideology by wiping out those who were advocates of moderation. Furthermore, the ideologues of Sindikuwabo's regime intended to involve as many people as possible in order to discourage them from testifying to the genocide for fear of implicating themselves. The slaughters and the destruction of holy symbols were mute testimony to the abject moral decay at all levels of Rwandese society, where injustice and impunity were rampant. Tabernacles, baptismal fonts, pulpits, vestments, crucifixes, statues, altars, Bibles and prayer books — all the sacred symbols and icons of religion — were slashed and damaged, leaving those who witnessed the deliberate desecration stunned by the extent of the rage which must have driven the violators. There are many reports of screaming victims being physically dragged to churches before being killed at the entrances.

In the upheavals of 1959, 1963, 1967, 1973 and 1990, religious workers had usually been spared, except for the occasional revenge or accidental killing. Even more soul-destroying was the fact that this time the killers were often trusted members of congregations. Protestant pastors were no exception, nor were religious sisters. Many parish priests and pastors were good shepherds who served their flock — a favourite symbol in Rwanda churches is Jesus as the good shepherd gently keeping a flock of sheep together with his pastoral staff — so why the brutality against those shepherds and the desecration of church buildings?

Most Rwandese Christians would agree with the "Surviving Church" that attempts to destroy the church responded to two basic and related situations: the extremely close ties of important church leaders to the Habyarimana regime, which compromised their prophetic voice and undermined completely their moral authority, and the deliberate intention of those organizing the genocide to destroy any voice of critique or dissent.

Despite the position of the leaders of the church, small movements existed within the churches which did work for justice, peace, human rights and democratization prior to April 6. However, they were simply too weak to counteract the ceaseless propaganda of the government. Indeed, those who did speak out were early targets of the militias. To be a credible voice of protest, the churches' leaders would have had to disengage themselves from close links to the ruling party and regime, which most of them were unable to do even after the genocide began.

The churches also had ethnic tensions of their own. For many years the church was perceived as one place in which Tutsis with ambitions to higher education and the professions might have been welcomed. Most of the leaders were Hutu, and it was difficult for Tutsi clergy to reach more senior positions. Many attacks on church compounds and religious workers were a result of the overall plan to eliminate Tutsis and moderate Hutus.

Ethnic identity is surfacing in many negative ways everywhere in the world today, not just in Africa. There are many reasons for it, including a reaction against over-centralized, corrupt and exploitative governments, a search for cultural identity amid the constant changes and confusion of modern society and alienation which threatens the very roots of community. In Africa, multi-party democracy is promoted — some would say imposed — by Western proponents of globalization. But it often breaks down along ethnic lines and quickly undermines already fragile nation states.

Within all the churches of Rwanda, ethnic tensions often surfaced at the time of elections or nominations to senior ecclesiastical positions. Splits were glossed over but never healed; people were elected, not for their spiritual, administrative or leadership qualities, but along ethnic lines. In some Anglican and Roman Catholic dioceses, the scandal of ethnic conflict split the clergy from the people. Indeed, the Anglican Church in Rwanda, with only about 100,000 members, has more dioceses than the Roman Catholics, simply to accommodate tensions, rather than healing them.

## Reluctant and martyred bishops

It cannot be underlined too strongly that there were many countless acts of heroism, even among some leaders, once they got over the shock of the murderous attacks on their once-sacred compounds. They hid and protected many thousands of people who might have been massacred, often at the price of their own lives and of their families. They did not ask for identity cards or enquire about denominational affiliation; they were prepared to live out gospel values to overcome historical ethnic divisions even if it meant martyrdom. They are the hope of a new and different church of tomorrow, able to speak to society with a credible and united voice, beyond ethnic tensions.

Besides his words during the special African synod, Pope John Paul spoke out again publicly when three Catholic bishops were killed in June by four RPF soldiers assigned to protect them in the major seminary at Kabgayi where they had fled early in the war. It was a serious blow to RPF's image of being committed to human rights and the rule of law. The rebels, already winning the war, moved quickly to minimize the damage, announcing openly on the radio that the killings were the responsibility of four youths — many of RPF's soldiers are teenagers who were "adopted" into the movement after losing their families in the genocide — who believed the bishops were to blame for the deaths of their parents. One of the teenage soldiers was killed and the three others were to have been brought to justice, but to date no word has been heard of their capture. RPF leaders have admitted they have no evidence that any of the bishops, who were shot as they ate their dinner, had participated in any killings.

The three were Archbishop Nsengiyumva, head of the Rwandese church and bishop of Kigali; Bishop Thaddée Nsengiyumva of Kabgayi (no relation to the archbishop, but a distant relative of Habyarimana), the president of the episcopal conference; and Bishop Joseph Ruzindana of Byumba. All were Hutu. Ten priests, including the vicar-general of Kabgayi, were also killed in the same massacre.

The pope deplored the killings, linking their deaths to the appalling situation in Rwanda and the endless series of atrocities against the people and churches. As few international church leaders were doing at the time, Pope John Paul urged decisive action by the international community to end the fighting in what he called "this martyred nation".

Few, even Catholics, have felt deeply the loss of Archbishop Nsengiyumva, although all church leaders condemn his assassination. He had been conspicuous, with his Anglican counterpart, in refusing to condemn the massacres, and headed a church which had never officially challenged the growing injustices of the government. Not so his namesake, Bishop Thaddée, who had worked closely since 1991 with the AACC and other ecumenically minded Christians to help mediate between government, opposition parties and the RPF.

Bishop Thaddée consistently opposed ethnic and regional discrimination in education, government jobs and business opportunities and became an outspoken critic of his church's ties to government, especially the archbishop's close relations with Habyarimana (the president had installed a direct telephone line between their two offices).

In an open letter on December 1, 1991, Bishop Thaddée had written that "the church is sick" because of its close ties to government, its silence on ethnic discrimination and unwillingness to negotiate a settlement of the war, begun a year earlier by the RPF. He also called for a transitional government, multiparty elections and a national convention. According to *African Rights*, the papal nuncio at the time, Archbishop Giuseppe Bertello, a staunch supporter of human rights in Rwanda, described the letter as "providential", but Archbishop Nsengiyumva was said to be furious.

In early 1992, Bishop Thaddée was instrumental in establishing and chairing an ecumenical committee of Catholics and

Protestants to work for peace and justice. It met with the RPF and participated fully in AACC initiatives to bring the various parties together, culminating in a meeting at Mombasa to show support for the Arusha Accords.

According to Nkusi, this initiative was strongly supported by Protestant pastors and Catholic priests, who found it gave them the support and confidence they needed to speak out against the extremists. Sadly, many of these outspoken clergy were among the first to be killed, notably the priests, monks and sisters at the Christus Centre on April 8.

On the other hand, the church leaders' response ranged from fury to silence to lukewarm support, which disappeared as pressure grew from the presidential mansion and the archbishop's palace after it became clear the Arusha Accords were not going to be implemented.

The Protestant and Anglican church leaders were less firmly tied to the presidency, except for Archbishop Nshamihigo, a former army chaplain who was a warm personal friend of the president and who remains unrepentant for his support of the extremists in the interim government. But the non-Catholic church leaders in general were just as unwilling to take courageous stands. Sources within these churches suggest that they had been bought off with presidential favours. Habyarimana's lavish patronage to those at the top of the churches certainly had many strings attached to it: for example, they were all expected to turn up dutifully at the airport for each presidential arrival and departure.

It took a while for the international media to catch up with the pattern of killings and desecration of churches after April 6 but when it did, newspapers and television concentrated on Archbishop Nshamihigo, perhaps because his Catholic counterpart was dead. Politically, in fact, there was little to distinguish the two in terms of their ardent and unquestioning support for Habyarimana, the MRND and, later, the interim government.

Headlines screamed: "Church of the Holy Slaughter" (*The Observer*); "Church fails to sever ties with killers" (*The Guardian*); "Rock That Broke: Rwanda's Church" (*New York Times*).

Archbishop Nshamihigo is not a good public relations person. Like many other church leaders, he would do well to learn from another Anglican leader, AACC president Desmond Tutu, who is honest with the media and conveys by his words and actions a transparency, integrity and charm that make him one of the world's great media stars. Moreover, Tutu understands that the church's mission requires it to communicate frankly and directly its message of justice and peace —even if the media are generally ecclesiastically illiterate and usually uninterested. He knows well that cover-ups and dissimulation usually backfire.

Under pressure, Nshamihigo's voice rises and he giggles, giving the impression that he is on the verge of hysteria. He is the subject of intense controversy; and several Anglican priests and lay people have told me they will never accept his leadership again because of his continuing close ties to the rump government based in eastern Zaire.

The archbishop first made headlines on June 3 when he and Bishop Jonathan Ruhumuliza of Kigali called a press conference in Nairobi en route to Britain and Canada to raise funds for their churches and to tell the world about the horrors of Rwanda. It was a public relations disaster. Nshamihigo, "smart in purple" (*The Observer*), handed out his business cards and began the press conference by blaming the crisis in Rwanda on the advancing RPF. He said he was not speaking to the press to condemn, but to explain.

"The RPF had planned in advance to kill their opponents. They had weapons to kill these people. This has become a big hindrance to the work of pacification by the interim government, the church and other peace-lovers."

Many of us who were present had already seen the mounds of corpses piled like matchsticks in church compounds, and the journalists pounced on the reference to the interim government as "peace-loving", demanding to know if the archbishop, as his country's senior churchman, would condemn the massacres clearly supported by the interim government.

He refused. "I don't want to condemn one group without condemning the other one," the archbishop said — just after he had condemned the RPF. At this point the journalists walked out, a rare occasion in Nairobi. Wiser heads prevailed during their fund-raising visits to London and Toronto, where the two were kept on a short media leash, although Nshamihigo claimed he was misquoted, then caught off-guard and finally that he was not familiar with English. In fact, he had spoken in French throughout the press conference.

Later in Goma, after the government had fallen and he had fled to a safer place, he was interviewed by *The Guardian's* well-respected Chris McGreal, who wrote that Archbishop Nshamihigo meets on a "regular basis" with those accused of mass murder, the members of the defunct government wanted by the UN for crimes against humanity.

He and some other Catholic and Anglican bishops and Protestant leaders are still reluctant to condemn those responsible for organizing the massacres and to name the killings as genocide.

But some church leaders in the camps are more outspoken. An Anglican official told me in Goma:

> We must build tolerance and allay the refugees' fears of Rwanda's new government. The wounds are deep. We will have to go step-by-step. It could take years. The militias are still very powerful in the camps and we will be killed if there is a confrontation. But people have to know that they did bad things, to repent and to make amends to the relatives of those they killed. They must accept that they did wrong and they must change their way of living.

This person, now working with CWA-R, cannot be identified for his own safety.

## Trying to bridge the gaps

The controversy around church leaders in all denominations is painful and extremely divisive. The AACC has worked from the beginning to bridge the gaps between leaders and followers and ethnic groups, and to help restore unity in a country that is still on the brink of disaster. On four different occasions it held "hearings" at its Nairobi headquarters, including one with Archbishop Tutu, to bring together Catholics, Protestants and evangelicals to begin the process of healing and reconciliation. Rwanda's church leaders in exile, including Archbishop Nshamihigo, were in attendance.

On September 30, at one of these hearings, Peter Lwaminda, general secretary of AMECEA, urged that reconciliation and consolidation of church and society within Rwanda itself was in the long term more important than the concentration of the worldwide church on humanitarian aid in Burundi, Tanzania and Zaire.

> People have to begin to understand the depth of their trauma if we are to have reconciliation. There must also be conditions inside the country to ensure the safe return of the refugees. Churches must work with patience and courage in the process of rebuilding trust and mutual acceptance, of moving from despair to hope, from misinformation to admitting the truth, from revenge and hatred towards forgiveness and reconciliation.

The bishops and their flocks who are outside Rwanda, however, feel insecure and afraid to return. Nshamihigo says he cannot in conscience suggest that people return because they may well be killed or arrested. Another Anglican said he was ready to return if the government would "guarantee" security and facilitate the return of the refugees, most of whom are now reasonably well fed, although camp security in Zaire and Tanzania remains poor. The bishops also insist they must remain with their people who have fled. They do not want to return alone, but when all the other Christian churches decide to go back.

Bishop Norman Kayumba of the Anglican diocese of Kigeme expressed hurt at being blamed by international media and church leaders for remaining outside Rwanda.

> Our fears are well-founded in fact. We know of many people who have returned and disappeared or come back wounded, reporting of revenge killings in the country. We condemn the killings. We have been suffering greatly, and we do not want a divided church. We appreciate your efforts to minister to both sections of the church, inside and outside.

Eleazar Ziherambere, legal representative of the Baptist Union of Rwanda, had similar worries. He wanted the healing process to be conducted in such a way as to bring together all Rwandese and "not hurt some of the people [refugees and exiles] it is expected to reconcile. Sometimes I think we have forgotten that those in exile and in the camps also need pastoral care and forgiveness. They need nurture too."

There is clearly no consensus. The government seems to want the moral vacuum filled by churches willing to take a different stance from the old church, but it is also clear that it does not want churches to have the kind of power they once held and abused. There are suggestions from senior RPF officials that some church leaders now in exile may face arrest if they return. At least one priest and three sisters are in the crowded prison in Kigali, held without charges and on hearsay evidence. Catholic leaders say attempts to have them released have so far been in vain. These are not conditions to encourage an early return from church leaders in exile.

On the other hand, the old church was close to moral bankruptcy at some strategic levels, and few deny it should be rebuilt at all levels. "If a country that is 90 percent Christian can act like this, what does it say about the church? What has led to these sorts of things? The church has to see what it did or did not do in that debased, immoral culture," said a missionary who left Rwanda April 12 in a truck convoy of expatriates. He added that the bishops had abused their power and diminished their moral authority, but he intends to return and support his remaining colleagues, hoping they may now be emboldened to regain their prophetic role "so that justice is the bedrock on which the future is formed".

Chipenda agrees.

> We have seen this moral vacuum, this lack of sufficient emphasis on justice in both Burundi and Rwanda. Churches must recover that commitment if they are to play any kind of role in bringing about peace and reconciliation. What concerns me, and causes me great agony, is that somehow we see well-intentioned people saying that humanitarian aid is some kind of substitute for justice.

Paradoxically, says Chipenda, the tragedy may have positive effects on the churches in Rwanda. There can be a chance for a dialogue and a Christianity that has been forced to mature through its suffering, one which is "profoundly African and liberated from old ways of doing things. It could point the way to the church of the future if it will first heal itself and its divisions."

Some say the old church demanded blind obedience and that Rwandese remained true to the old ideas of monarchy. According to Laurien Ntezimana, a lay theologian from the Roman Catholic diocese of Butare,

> Rwandese know how to obey but they do not know how to dialogue. Political opponents or people who disagree are considered above all as enemies. Democracy has not yet penetrated our minds. The church has always exalted the virtue of obedience, and if you talk to ordinary people they will tell you that many of the massacres happened because they blindly obeyed the authorities, regardless of who they were or how evil they were.

A church of the future preoccupies Chipenda and his colleagues at AACC much more than does the future of the church. Responding to the sense of abandonment felt by the "Surviving Church", AACC staff have developed the broad outlines of this church of the future, facing up to the questions of what went wrong, why the church failed to be prophetic, why people allowed themselves to fall into blind obedience or co-option, how to deal with grief and healing. According to Setri Nyomi, who heads the AACC Christian and Family Life Education desk:

> This church needs to be radically different from the church which was paralyzed because it was too tied to political powers to be prophetic. It was unable to be a reconciling force at the time when Rwanda was entangled in bitter divisions and hatred. The church (leaders and all) as it was before the war was implicated in the atrocities. The church as church, as well as individual Christians, saw their identity more terms of the ethnic divide or the political divide.

Some of the elements Nyomi sees in the church of the future in both Rwanda and Africa are:
— seeking God's will in times such as this, even if this will is radically different from the tendencies surrounding us (hatred, division, self-seeking actions, murder);
— empathy with those who are suffering, taking a lead in the healing that needs to take place (emotionally, physically, spiritually) by providing humanitarian aid and standing with the church in time of need;
— being a leading force in the process of healing, reconciliation, peace and justice;
— being part of the rebuilding of a new Rwanda;
— being faithful in our witness no matter where we are.

This is the basis for a process of healing that must occur if Rwanda is to return to justice, peace and reconciliation. But as yet there are large numbers of Catholic and a smaller number of Protestant clergy, especially in the refugee camps, who seem unwilling to take the first step, which is repentance. *African Rights* lists the names of thirty Rwandese Catholic priests in Zaire who will return with their people only if certain conditions are met. These include what amounts to a blanket amnesty, the end of any plan for an international tribunal to judge war criminals, full participation of all political parties, including the parties of the killers, and reintegration of the FAR into a national army.

Similar situations exist in Tanzania, according to German pastor Jörg Zimmermann, who says that while he witnessed many acts of genuine personal faith, there was little sign that the churches accepted any responsibility for the tragedy or were reflecting about the root causes of the genocide. People were uncomfortable about questions and tended in general to blame the RPF for provoking and harassing people.

The church in Rwanda can no longer afford to be divided. Bold measures are required, including determining what solidarity means in the context of the rest of Africa and the ecumenical movement worldwide. Silence will be seen as acquiescence. Repentance and rebirth will mean a new nation and a new church.

## CWA-R: an ecumenical response

Church World Action-Rwanda was born out of the tragedy and may well point to a new way of churches responding to crises. Before CWA-R was formed in May 1994, the WCC and AACC had together visited Rwanda to explain and support the Arusha Accords and convened a consultation on peace and reconciliation in November 1993 in Mombasa.

CWA-R became operational when the refugees flocked into Tanzania. On May 19 it issued the first of several financial appeals to respond to the emergency. In its conceptualization this joint initiative by the LWF and WCC went beyond mere humanitarian aid to include spiritual and reconciliation components and the need for improved communications:

In the face of the tragedy in Rwanda, and the difficulties being encountered by surrounding countries, the action of the churches and church-related agencies worldwide needs to be co-ordinated and rapid. The presence of the churches witnessing for tolerance and peace, demonstrating international concern through humanitarian assistance and promoting reconciliation through crisis support is the focus of this joint ecumenical appeal.

The words were something the African churches wanted and needed to hear: that they were not to be alone, but would be an integral part of a co-ordinated response which would address their concerns about the root causes of the killings, the apparent failures of churches in Rwanda, their belief that solutions to Africa's problems must be long-term and African, their frustration at lack of consultation and cultural insensitivity.

CWA-R combined the professional operational experience of the LWF with the WCC's concerns for justice, peace and reconciliation. It brought together partners from the North, like Dutch Interchurchaid and Christian Aid, with AACC, TCRS and, until it was destroyed, the CPR. It was a first, a kind of experiment in ecumenical response, and the jury is still out on its effectiveness.

There could hardly have been a more difficult disaster in which to launch a new initiative such as CWA-R. Rwanda shook the international aid-relief-emergency-humanitarian community to the core. The self-examination and recrimination now going on around the world about the clear inability of anyone to stop the tragedy and deal with what the UN has finally called "concerted, planned, systematic and methodical genocide" show that forty years of experience in dealing with disasters had severe shortcomings.

Warning flags were raised long before April 6. Church leaders in Nairobi tried to warn that Habyarimana was not serious about the Arusha Accords. Others of course remained silent as he prepared to implement the "final solution".

Joining hands with the UNHCR and the horde of NGOs that poured into Rwanda and nearby countries may not have been what the churches envisaged, but the magnitude of the refugee exodus was unparalleled. Statistically, the relief effort to Rwanda was rather impressive. Several hundreds of millions of dollars of aid, including US$21 million from CWA-R, was poured into the camps on short notice, but the million or so refugees are still there in reasonably good health; indeed, many are better off than they were before they were forced to flee. Food, medicines, shelter and logistical support moved into Goma and Benaco quite well despite the difficult circumstances. CWA-R was one of the early operational humanitarian agencies in both places.

The problem, as noted earlier, is that among the refugees are the killers, using the aid as a tool to rebuild their army and using food aid and other threats to keep people from going home. Rwanda has proved in stark terms that there is no such thing as "neutral" humanitarian aid. Here is a major dilemma that must be addressed by all international agencies, not just CWA-R. However, given the moral and ethical dimensions which churches should be at the forefront of debating, the ecumenical movement needs to rethink how easy it is to follow the herd, using modern communications technologies to raise large amounts of money without too much thought about the implications of what that money is being used for. As the debate on the failure of humanitarian aid in Rwanda to do what it was supposed to do heats up, the people in the pews who contribute may also have questions about what they give to in the future. Credibility is at stake, but there is a larger issue: should churches respond instantly to CNN before their partners on the ground can provide their analysis of the situation? Should there not always be a moment of reflection about where this generosity is leading?

As Chipenda keeps repeating, the issue is justice, old-fashioned biblical justice, not simply fund-raising, as important as that is in practical terms. Solutions must be grappled with, and they are less easy to raise money for.

Refugee co-ordinators suggest that the camps in Zaire and Tanzania may need to remain at least through 1995. Some of the biggest agencies have already withdrawn in protest against the violence and insecurity of the camps, but as one leaves, there are many more to take its place. And while refugees outside Rwanda are reasonably well off, the lives of the internally displaced within the country are a misery, and the government, undemocratic as it may be, limps along with almost no resources and little control of the basic instruments of governance like security for its people and the rule of law. Many relief officials fear that a full-scale return of refugees in the immediate future would destabilize the country even further.

CWA-R shares this frustration and has committed itself to going much further than just feeding the hungry. "It will be there long after the emergency, with the churches and the people of Rwanda," says Myra Blyth, director of the WCC's programme unit on Sharing and Service.

At a meeting in Geneva in October, CWA-R noted "significant progress" in aiding the refugees but declared that the situation in Rwanda was "so insecure and unstable" that the refugees could not return. It criticized the UN for failing to take adequate action to protect the refugees, a charge the UN promptly denied.

Eight months after the outbreak of the crisis, said CWA-R, virtually none of the measures proposed by the UN regarding the human rights situation had been implemented. CWA-R is also worried that the lack of funds for the international tribunal to identify and prosecute war criminals leaves the way open for summary trials by the unelected government, which has no functioning judiciary in place.

CWA-R has set up offices in Goma and Kigali, whose main job is to work on the humanitarian concerns. Visits by WCC and LWF staff are fairly regular, but liaison with local churches is a steady source of tension. A crisis support programme known as ACIST (African Community Initiatives Support Programme), set up to respond to the individual psychological and spiritual needs of Rwandese caught in the aftermath of the genocide, has been slow to get off the ground. It is essentially a project to help the most seriously affected — orphans, widows, rape victims, the severely traumatized — while church and community structures, which should normally undertake such work, can be rebuilt. ACIST is planned as a participatory process using local partners and member churches in Rwanda and the refugee camps along with expatriate experts in conflict resolution.

Another element of CWA-R's mandate is peace and reconciliation, led by the AACC, a process which is fraught with concern and some misunderstanding. Because so many Rwandese are outside, including many of the church leaders and pastors, the peace and reconciliation process must focus both inside and out. There is pressure on the refugees to return home from the Kigali government, the UN and most aid agencies. The refugees resolutely refuse, claiming there is inadequate security, and the church leaders who remain in the camps insist they are simply staying with their people during this hour of need. As Rwanda slowly resumes some modest form of normality, "Surviving Church" leaders argue for a return of their bishops and presidents and moderators, but security conditions, while improving, are not sufficient to persuade those who should return home to come back.

The AACC has asked the new government several times to improve security and to sort out the problem of property rights which is a major bone of contention. People who return to Kigali to find someone else living in their houses have no adequate way of seeking recompense or repossessing what is rightfully theirs. There are "private acts of justice" going on all the time, a UN monitor told churches recently, along with daily acts of minor violence. But, adds Reetta Leskinen of Finland, this has to be seen in the context of what went on before under a government which systematically massacred people.

Added to these problems are the looting and damage done to churches and housing, destruction of records and a severe shortage of funds.

## No easy reconciliation

One can easily understand Chipenda's insistence that peace and reconciliation is a process that will take many years, not a project that can be completed in six months.

The most immediate and severe need, however, is to help Rwandese cope with the psychological and spiritual results of the bloodshed.

"This problem did not happen overnight," says Chipenda, "and it will not be resolved overnight. The world did not listen when we called for help earlier, and sometimes it seems to me it is not listening now. If we were helpless in the face of genocide, how are we going to effect peace and reconciliation now, when there is no real emphasis on justice?"

The AACC general secretary notes that church life has again begun to "flourish" despite the absence of leaders. As people meet to worship ecumenically, "they find solace and strength in their frequent meetings". Lay people, parish priests and pastors have assumed leadership roles.

The reality, however, is that there are Rwandese living outside the country in large numbers and there are Rwandese inside the country, many who have returned after years of exile in Uganda, Zaire and Burundi. There are armies inside and outside. There are politicians at home and in exile. There are church leaders at home and in exile. From a reconciliation perspective, these are realities which must somehow be dealt with justly.

It cannot be an easy reconciliation, given the depths of hatred and anger church delegations observe in the over-crowded and highly politicized refugee camps and the equal insistence inside the country that those responsible for the genocide be brought to justice quickly before frustration leads to a wider outbreak of revenge-killings. This is why African churches insist that human rights monitors are needed and the international tribunal must start its work immediately inside Rwanda.

Chipenda says that "the conditions simply do not exist in Rwanda where we can begin dialogue in a formal way between these many diverse elements, most of whom do not trust one another and who have not yet come to terms, spiritually and emotionally, with the depths of their suffering".

The AACC also believes that the peace and reconciliation process must be much more African in its outlook and direction, using traditional means of conflict resolution, with a goal of providing a church that is much more Rwandan in character and less dependent on northern theology, liturgy, polity and ethos.

Chipenda likens the instability of the country to the vol-canoes near Goma. "They could erupt any time... We have to be careful not to create further instability and polarization. We have to facilitate dialogue with all the various realities inside and outside the country, and we have to do it in a manner which *shows* that justice is being done."

CWA-R and AACC cannot impose reconciliation on Rwanda or its churches. They can promote dialogue, support justice and disseminate information, but ultimately the conflict must be resolved within the country.

President Pasteur Bizimungo and Prime Minister Faustin Twagiramungo make clear they want reconciliation and that they see a key role for the churches in effecting long-term change in the moral and ethical climate of Rwanda. "Right now, the government is doing your work," the prime minister told an AACC delegation. "We should not be the moral custodians of people's lives. It is the churches of Rwanda who must fill that role. The only thing we insist upon is that those who planned and carried out the genocide must not be allowed impunity." But he also stressed that justice would be done within internationally acceptable standards and openly before the whole world.

The emphasis on long-term African solutions within the reality of a divided church and people has at times caused misunderstandings between CWA-R and AACC. Although difficult, these are well worth working out together, says Chipenda, and CWA-R staff and AACC have discussed at some length their different understandings of whom they are serving. After a pastoral visit to Rwanda in late November, the AACC general secretary summarized these concerns and made some proposals for closer co-operation and understanding. "AACC emphasizes the collaborative nature of the CWA-R mandate," he said, "noting in particular that peace and reconciliation is not a distinct project, but a process which infuses the whole ecumenical undertaking in Rwanda and the region."

Churches in Rwanda have been devastated both spiritually and structurally. Many leaders and members are dead or in exile. There are almost no resources other than community and worship. CWA-R staff has access to funds, logistics and communications.

Some pastors inside Rwanda feel isolated from CWA-R because they do not understand its mandate, nor how it is being implemented. They told the AACC delegation that they had the impression that somehow their needs do not fit CWA-R criteria, and that the only immediate services available to them have been communications facilities — fax and telephone — for which they expressed gratitude.

On a regional level, the AACC has already established a process of consultation and collaboration with AMECEA and the Association of Evangelicals in Africa (AEA) and other church-related groups to address the churches' role in facing the long-term implications of the Rwanda tragedy on neighbouring countries. Chipenda sees the situation in Rwanda as so serious and volatile that "it could easily destabilize the whole sub-region. There is too much mistrust, too much polarization, too many weapons and too little political dialogue at the moment; and we fear military responses to what are essentially political problems."

While CWA-R struggles to fulfil its mandate in Kigali and Goma, there has been a proliferation of US-based right-wing evangelical relief organizations who seem to be using the misery of Rwanda's people to swell their own coffers. Operation Blessing, supported by television evangelist and politician Pat Robertson, has appeared in Goma with "medical missionaries" working in a small clinic which, mainstream agencies say, has far more evangelists than doctors. The UN accuses Operation Blessing of refusing help to people who are not willing to take "a healthy dose of religion along with their medicine".

Dozens of other right-wing fundamentalist groups have launched massive television appeals for large donations to "help" Rwanda. Says UN medical co-ordinator Claire Bourgeois, "Operation Blessing is no longer under UN co-ordination. Personally speaking, I don't think they should use health care to reach people to teach them religion. Most of the people in the camps already have strong church affiliations."

The use of misery to raise funds has a tendency to confuse both individual and corporate donors in the North as well as the recipients in the camps and in Rwanda itself. Mainstream church agencies are incredulous about the figure of 149 international agencies registered with the government. No more than twenty are visible, they say, which raises the question of what the rest of them are doing. Herbie Cullen of the Irish medical charity Goal describes a tiny Irish agency which spent "thousands of pounds to fly out three people with a few bags of drugs. I think they just used Rwanda to raise money so they could fly out," he told *The Guardian*.

The UN has no authority over these agencies, some of whom arrive promising to do feasibility assessments on one or more aspects of the tragedy. "They run around with hand-held video cameras taking metres of film, much of it at emergency sites already established by major agencies, and then disappear," says the manager of a camp for displaced people inside Rwanda. "The next thing we hear of them is that they have been raising funds with these videos. But very little of it ever gets back here." AACC was told of one agency which arrived with the stated purpose of "educating" people about land mines. When someone asked, "Who will remove the mines?" the reply was, "We don't know. That is someone else's job."

One of the biggest and most controversial aspects of the response to the Rwanda emergency concerns orphans, for whom it is of course particularly easy to raise funds. The government has accused several agencies of taking children away from relatives and friends in villages to camps or, in a few cases, sending them overseas to adoption agencies, which is illegal.

\* \* \*

The November 1993 Mombasa consultation had as its theme "On the Search for a Lasting Peace in Rwanda". More than half of the people who attended that three-day meeting of political and religious leaders are now dead. Many more are in exile.

The message from Mombasa urged politicians and parties to put national interest ahead of partisan and personal interests and to use dialogue rather than violence to resolve conflict. It called on citizens to practise tolerance, respect others' views and refuse to be manipulated by those who refuse reconciliation. It said churches should act as the moral guardians of society and not become enmeshed in political partisanship. And it called on the international community to help implement the Arusha Accords and to make resources available for the rehabilitation of refugees and displaced persons.

This message was widely distributed just four months before April 6, 1994. It was never implemented. It is the same call which must be made once again — to politicians, citizens, church leaders and the international community — if Rwanda is to avoid another looming disaster and return its people to their homes and fields in justice and in safety. It is a call that must come clearly and universally from Africa and the North, from churches and from the international community. It must come soon: the time is short.

# 6. Rwanda's Recovery: A Race with Time

It is a situation almost no one wishes to contemplate. It is too complicated, too distressing, too horrible. We do not want to see those pictures again. If only the pictures would go away, we could forget and move on to other crises. Yet, almost without looking, we sense the stark possibility of their coming back. The genocide could return now that we have admitted officially it actually happened.

To say that Rwanda is not a country the world sees as "important" and that there is an international reluctance to assume new responsibilities for it is an understatement of some proportions. But the consequences of turning away now, when the crisis could go either way, are also too awful to contemplate. The human consequences are more death and much more suffering. The political consequences are further instability in the region, further demands on an already beleaguered UN, further marginalization of Africa. The moral consequences go to the very centre of our humanity and to our most basic beliefs in justice — that we are responsible for our sisters and brothers wherever they may be and whatever their origins. Rwanda, having once shocked the world into belated action, cannot be left alone, half-populated, half-dead, to deal with its demons just because we are afraid to deal with the implacable problems lurking on the edge of our limited horizons.

The genocide planned by Habyarimana's Network Zero, implemented by Sindikubwabo's interim government of extremists and ended by Kagame's Rwandan Patriotic Front when it formed a government on July 19 has now been verified by a Commission of Experts named by the UN. Three African jurists delivered their report to Boutros-Ghali on December 3:

> After careful deliberation, the Commission of Experts has con-
> cluded that there exists overwhelming evidence to prove that acts
> of genocide against the Tutsi group were perpetrated by Hutu
> elements in a planned, systematic and methodical way.

That statement should put the debate to rest, despite the reluctance of the Security Council to act on the genocide and despite the attempts by Hutu extremists to rewrite history by passing the blame to the RPF. While the commission reported that soldiers from both armies had committed "serious breaches of international humanitarian law", it was unable to uncover "any evidence to indicate that members of the Tutsi minority perpetrated acts with intent to destroy the Hutu ethnic group as such".

The region is so tense — especially in Rwanda but also in Zaire, Burundi and, to a lesser extent, Tanzania — that a conflagration could be created by the smallest spark, whether ignited by a mistake, a misunderstanding or a miscalculation, to say nothing of a deliberate act of war by either side.

## Continuing disarray

When the RPF swept to victory in July, it took over a country in which there had been a deliberate and almost successful attempt to re-engineer an entire society based according to the blueprint of ethnicity. In such a society, every single surviving Hutu would have had blood on his or her hands. Everyone would have been implicated in the genocide. This is why the RPF says it refused to negotiate with the Sindikubwabo regime during the hundred-day war, because it would have meant prolonging the genocide and talking with a killer regime which never acknowledged it was doing anything wrong. The RPF insisted, as did the Allies in the second world war, on an unconditional victory. What it does with that victory now is probably the critical question for the future of Rwanda. The second most critical issue is the responsibility of the international community to ensure that the RPF lives up to its promises and has the resources to do so. On both of these points there is little reason for optimism in either the short or the long term.

In addition to taking over a depopulated country whose infrastructure is badly damaged, whose treasury was thoroughly looted and moved to Zaire and whose population is severely polarized, the new government has come under heavy pressure from Europe and North America to limit the war crimes trials to a few token leaders and to form a government of national unity including members of the MRND and even the CDR.

The Twagiramungu government has flatly refused to include people it regards as genocidal killers and points out that more than half of its 19 members are already from other, Hutu-dominated parties. It also insists there can be no reconciliation and rehabilitation without bringing the most serious killers to trial, conviction and sentencing, a position with which the international community agrees, at least in theory. The UN has dusted off its 1951 Genocide Convention, to which Rwanda is a signatory, which has remained unused since the end of the Nuremberg trials of Nazi war criminals. The RPF-led government says it will turn over the ringleaders of the massacres to an international tribunal.

The Kigali government says it wants the refugees to return, that they are safe and that revenge killings by the undisciplined teenagers who make up the bulk of the unpaid 30,000-member Rwandan Patriotic Army (the military wing of the RPF) will be controlled. The RPF, which has one of the most effective intelligence wings in Africa outside South Africa, knows that the hardliners who organized the genocide control the refugee camps and are actively training to stage a guerilla war. They view pressure to widen the base of their government as an attempt to put extremists back into power.

Kigali is in a serious bind. Money from international sources, needed to begin establishing the basics of a government, has been extremely slow in coming. Some money was released by the European Union to rehabilitate wrecked water and electricity plants in the capital, and just before the end of 1994 the World Bank agreed to release part of the US$250 million it has promised, conditional on Rwanda repaying its arrears of some US$8 million (no one knows where it is supposed to get that money). The EU is holding up some US$450 million in support payments because of French and Belgian insistence on better security for the refugees.

Four months after it took power, the new government still had no paid civil servants, no files, no computers, no tax revenue, no judges or police, few functioning offices, one grossly overcrowded prison and an empty treasury. Unpaid soldiers, ministers and functionaries are of course easy prey for corruption: already one minister made off with US$200,000 designated for the hard-pressed UN mission in New York.

Rwanda has always relied heavily on foreign aid. Now it is completely dependent on international agencies for peace-keeping, clearing mines, restoring schools and hospitals, caring for orphans, rebuilding the infrastructure, monitoring human rights and preparing for a war crimes tribunal — to say nothing of supporting some two million refugees outside its borders, which the UN estimates has already cost more than US$400 million.

The government in Kigali, dominated by the highly disciplined Kagame and his English-speaking RPF colleagues, is of course unelected. Moreover, it seems to have lost the capacity for good public relations which it displayed during the war, and it has alienated some of its more moderate supporters within the government and outside the country. Rumours persist that Hutus in the government are often not aware of policy decisions and directives until after they are implemented and that the less democratic elements of the government, the military, have shown little enthusiasm about human rights and the rule of law.

One of the government's best assets is Twagiramungu, the man who was supposed to have been prime minister once the Arusha Accords had been implemented. He is disgusted with the lack of support from the world community, which, he says, is playing into the hands of the extremists in Zaire and Tanzanian camps. "They're putting the cart before the horse," he says angrily. "How can we prove our good faith when they don't give us the means? If we had the resources to restore the administration, we could send the army back to its bases and reassure the refugees they can return."

One of the most contentious issues which the RPF-dominated government has refused to deal with is what the army has done to Hutus who have returned, especially the seizing of property and homes, the exercise of "summary justice" and the protection rackets run by the unpaid youthful soldiers. These stories are documented, but exaggerated versions of them run rampant through the camps, embellished by the powerful propaganda machine of the former government and its supporters.

Property, especially that owned by people who have died or who refuse to return from the camps, has been seized by army officers or, more commonly, by Tutsis returning from their many years in exile who grab an empty house as their own with no compensation, thus far, for the rightful owners. A new law is now in place protecting disputed property and submitting it to arbitration. But often the army colludes with the squatters and fails to evict them even when official papers are produced. Indeed, there are reports that Hutus asking for their property back have been arrested on the dubious ground that anyone who had property must have been close to the Habyarimana regime. Other Hutus are afraid to even claim their property, let alone occupy it.

People are routinely jailed — as many as 12,000, according to some human rights monitors — on trumped-up charges of being killers. Since there is no system for investigating charges or bringing the accused to trial, they languish in the one prison, built for 2000 inmates but now holding nearly five times that many, or in places where the army can keep them while the aid agencies feed them. One-third of Kigali's population of 200,000 came from Uganda, Burundi or Tanzania, where they had lived in exile for last 30 or more years, while Hutus who have returned cannot live in their houses.

The ragged army is being taught discipline, says Colonel Andrew Rwigamba. But he adds that most of the young soldiers saw their families wiped out, and it is not easy to impress upon them the need for restraint. They are also deeply frustrated by the inertia of the UN investigations into the perpetrators of the massacres and the endless delays in establishing an international tribunal. For people whose families have been wiped out and who have the means at hand to execute summary justice, that may be understood if not condoned.

Human rights monitors are scarce, with fewer than 50 covering the entire country. They are short of vehicles, communications equipment and experience. Many are young university graduates with little knowledge of Africa or Rwanda, and because of inadequate security they often fear to leave Kigali. Some cannot even speak French, let alone Kinyarwanda.

The few who are functioning say there is increasing evidence of executions without trial, personal acts of revenge and banditry and disappearances. Church workers in refugee camps report a "reign of terror" in the rural areas of Rwanda, far away from the monitors. The problem for journalists, monitors and the UNAMIR soldiers who are supposed to investigate such episodes is that these allegations of violence are all hearsay and cannot be verified by hard evidence. Nevertheless, these reports are widely circulated and sincerely believed by the refugees and are used as a tool by those who have a vested interest in keeping the Hutus outside the country. The sooner resources are put in place to establish a system of justice, including a civilian-controlled police and court system, the better. Not only could this serve to assure returnees that they will be safe, but it could also exonerate those who feel they have been condemned by the world without a hearing.

## Anarchy in the camps

When the Security Council voted on December 1 to renew the UNAMIR mandate for another six months (until June 9, 1995), it refused under US pressure to establish a separate force to provide security in the turbulent camps in Zaire. The US, apparently unmindful of the suffering and deaths that happened while it was delaying deployment of UNAMIR-II for almost two months, suggested that the UN should consider hiring private security companies in Zaire to patrol the camps and keep order — in the face of clear admission that the camps were under the control of the militias and former government. The Security Council debated whether sufficient troops — three to five thousand were proposed by the secretary-general — could be found.

US ambassador Madeleine Albright raised precisely the same questions she had brought up during the debate on UNAMIR-II. She wanted a detailed account of "the objectives, rules of engagement and precise costs of such an operation". She told the diplomats, most of whom fell in line with her reservations, that she thought the peace-keepers already present in Rwanda could carry out these additional responsibilities "within existing resources for the moment". The mandate of UNAMIR-II does not include policing the camps. Only Aotearoa New Zealand took exception to the Council's position, arguing that a UN police force was required, not more soldiers or private guards. Ambassador Colin Keating said it was urgent physically to separate genuine refugees from the political leaders of the former government and its soldiers and militias, both for their own safety and to give them space to decide for themselves whether or not to return without facing coercion and violence.

In the camps Zairean soldiers, unpaid themselves, loot the refugees' few belongings. The refugees in turn attack the soldiers with stones. The former government distributes food relief, using it as a weapon for achieving its own ends. So severe is the situation that at least 15 major agencies have withdrawn from Katale camp and are considering complete withdrawal because of threats and intimidation. Agencies also wrestle with the ethical question of feeding soldiers of the former Hutu extremist government so they can prepare their invasion and continue to terrorize the refugees into remaining in Zaire.

There is no overall practical prospect for a genuine settlement of this tragic situation. The refugees' awareness of this fuels the sense of mistrust and fear and spawns growing acts of violence and revenge. This is to the advantage of the former government, which has now established, according to eyewitness reports, two training camps some 50 kilometres from Bukavu where soldiers and new recruits are being whipped into shape to invade Rwanda and "finish" their job. Most observers feel it will be more a guerilla-type operation than conventional warfare. General Augustin Bizimungu, chief of staff of the exiled Hutu army, refers to the next stages of the war as an *intifada*, modelled on the Palestinian uprising in the West Bank and Gaza.

Kagame is not expected to stand idly by waiting for hostilities to break out. He has already said that guerilla activities are underway in the former French-protected zone, blaming them rather than his own troops for a spate of civilian massacres in the southwest corner of Rwanda. UNAMIR confirms the killings of more than 100 people but is uncertain who the perpetrators have been. Kagame was also quoted in radio interviews about the possibility of taking pre-emptive action by invading Eastern Zaire to "neutralize" the former regime. The political consequences of such an action would be extremely serious.

For these reasons some diplomats in the region have raised a hitherto almost taboo subject: the possibility of placing Rwanda under a UN mandate for a limited period of time to provide security, rebuild the shattered economy and infrastructure, assist in instituting a rule of law, bring home the refugees and prepare for democratic elections within five years.

A Kenyan diplomat who wishes to remain anonymous explained that the idea has been floated — more for reaction than immediate implementation — because of fears that the entire sub-region will be drawn into conflict. He says another war in Rwanda would not only render any attempts at reconciliation impossible for a long time but also polarize the fragile political balance in east and central African countries. Uganda is one of the staunchest supporters of the new government. Zaire's President Mobutu had a close relationship with Habyarimana and supports the former government. Indeed, Habyarimana's remains have been buried at Mobutu's home in Gbadolite until the situation "normalizes" and they can be returned to Rwanda. Burundi is extremely volatile. Tanzania is host to many thousands of Hutu refugees who show no signs of returning home. Sudan, wracked by its own long-running civil war, is alleged to be supporting a rebel movement in northern Uganda. While Kenya maintains a neutral position on Rwanda, a large number of exiles from both sides of the conflict are living in Nairobi. Somalia has no functioning government; and Ethiopia and Eritrea are struggling out of war and drought.

Reaction to the mandate idea, with its overtones of recolonization, is mixed. RPF officials angrily dismiss the entire notion as an "insulting" effort to undermine attempts to institute the rule of law by the new government of national unity. It has made a commitment to free and non-ethnic elections in five years, although it is difficult to see how, facing a huge Hutu majority, it could actually win at the ballot box without building in some constitutional minority guarantees. There are suggestions that powerful persons in France and Belgium with the ability to influence the European Union and the World Bank are behind the mandate idea. Other governments are silent, preoccupied as they are with their own internal problems.

The former government has not been asked its opinion, but it wants to fight, or pressure, its way back into at least a power-sharing relationship by including the political parties blamed for the genocide in the new government and restructuring the national army to include elements of the FAR.

## Justice for the victims

To attempt peace and reconciliation processes within this highly polarized political scene is virtually impossible, especially when the need for justice is so self-evident to one side and so totally rejected by the other. The international community cannot seem to find the will or the resources to do much more than try to maintain the status quo, which almost everyone but the UN Security Council feels is unsustainable.

The RPF insists that peace and reconciliation attempts can be effective only within the context of justice created by the international tribunal agreed upon by the UN membership. It fears that giving in to external pressures to include the former government will carry with it amnesty and reduce the horror of genocide to something like manslaughter. In October the new government prepared a strongly worded document entitled *Genocide in Rwanda: Genesis, Foundations and Magnitude*, which issued a stern warning to the UN not to delay the investigations and trials. The document rejects outright the arguments of the exiled government that the killings were the result of spontaneous grief at Habyarimana's death which the interim government could not control because it was too busy fighting the RPF attack.

> Such argument reduces a well-prepared and executed genocide to a manslaughter type of crime, thereby apologizing for the decades-old impunity in our country. The foundation for national reconciliation is fairness to all (justice). The trial of the perpetrators of the genocide is the only assurance to the victims of the genocide and a warning that no one can any longer kill at will and get away with it. It is a practical demonstration of commitment to a fresh start, based on the rule of law...
>
> Therefore the apparent reluctance of the international community to act fast on this question of genocide is regrettable. The delay in setting up tribunals to try the perpetrators of the genocide will only serve to create further tensions in the country, thereby complicating the question of national reconciliation. The continuation of a cynical attitude over the tragedy in Rwanda by the international community *may remind Rwandese of their own responsibility to put their country in order*, but may also evoke racial interpretations of the behaviour of the international community, especially the latter's principal agency, the United Nations (*italics added*).

Contrast this with statements by refugee leaders in Zaire that the Kigali government and the UN should "stop talking about an international tribunal where there is a risk that criminals will be, at the same time, both accusers and judges".

The denial of any wrongdoing which permeates the refugee camps is discouraging. The blame for their plight lies with someone else: the RPF, the Tutsis, the UN, the aid agencies. No one admits that the massacres were wrong. The old notion of impunity is still deeply engrained.

The RPF has objected to certain aspects of the international tribunal but has said it will co-operate fully. It cannot understand why the international community is so much more obsessed with the refugee crisis than with justice for the victims of genocide. Despite veiled threats to go ahead with the trials itself, Rwanda lacks the judicial system to do so. Its justice minister acknowledges this and has urged that personnel and resources be made available immediately. But by the end of 1994 only five of the needed two hundred field officers had been appointed and one of them resigned in protest at the lack of such basic equipment as vehicles, phones, offices and faxes.

There is also a considerable degree of frustration in deciding who should be tried. Some argue for only a token trial of the top leadership; others say it should be at least the planners and major killers. Twagiramungu at one stage proposed that every killer be tried, though he has since modified that, saying that it would be too long a process to bring some 32,000 people before the courts. At the least, however, most survivors inside Rwanda say all members of the interim government, senior politicians, propagandists, army, police, *interahamwe* and local officials must be arrested and tried. Since these are the people who control the refugee camps, it is little wonder that they do not wish to return.

The OAU has supported the idea since May, saying such trials were needed if Rwanda was to be healed, but also that they would serve as a warning to other perpetrators of similar despicable crimes and as a deterrent to those driven by revenge to institute summary executions because of the delay in bringing about justice.

While there are many unanswered questions about the process of the tribunal, the single greatest barrier to justice is the inertia and procrastination of the UN. It has formally expanded the Yugoslavian tribunal established in The Hague under South Africa's Judge Richard Goldstone to include the Rwanda genocide. Goldstone made one quick visit to Kigali, but little else has been accomplished and very little of the estimated US$16 million needed to bring in investigators and prosecutors has been forthcoming. Massacre sites have not been visited and very few witnesses have been interviewed. Yet *African Rights* has been able to talk to hundreds of witnesses, compiling horrific accounts of what happened and naming scores of suspects.

There is real concern that evidence will disappear and witnesses will be intimidated or begin to forget some of their most vivid recollections. Many Rwandese also fear that justice will be put aside in the name of peace and reconciliation and history rewritten in the name of preserving unity. Twagiramungu called it "incomprehensible" that countries like France and the US should propose amnesty or negotiations with the old regime before those responsible are brought to trial. "As we speak, there are still people trying to track down Nazis around the world 50 years after the second world war. Can Rwanda somehow be different?"

There have been many crimes committed in Rwanda and in the neighbouring camps: massacres, torture, rape, robbery with violence, looting, revenge slayings, stealing property, common theft. The list is endless, but the overriding crime of genocide is the one which cannot be explained away. It cannot be the subject of amnesty. It cannot be ignored in the name of reconciliation; and if it is, through lack of will or lack of resources, then the hideous crimes the world has witnessed will have been done with impunity and the dead will surely cry out from their mass graves.

\* \* \*

Genocide is the most notorious crime against humanity recognized by international law. It is deliberate murder born of the myth that one ethnic group, race or creed is superior to another and that it is thus legitimate to eliminate that "other" to gain power. After Hitler's death camps shocked the world, the Genocide Convention signed by most countries obliged signatory states to do certain specified things to prevent and punish it.

Until now, the record has been poor. Charges have never been brought against Pol Pot's regime in Cambodia, where a million people were killed, or against Iraq for its oppression of

Kurds, or against the succession of murderous regimes in Haiti or against the apartheid rulers of South Africa. The Genocide Convention makes it clear that any deliberate attempt to harm a national, ethnic, racial or religious group is a crime against humanity even if, as in many of the cases mentioned, it is committed by a government against its own people within its own boundaries. Rwanda clearly fits this description.

In most cases genocide proceedings have not been instituted because of a lack of political will or an inability to find the criminals. Peace negotiations or ceasefires are often negotiated — for example, in Haiti and South Africa — with an understanding that amnesty will be granted. In Rwanda, there was no negotiated ceasefire and there has been no amnesty. If the UN can get its act together, the tragedy of Rwanda, with the perpetrators no longer in power and the government willing to co-operate, may be the object lesson needed for the world to set a precedent telling the growing fascist movements around the world that genocide will not go unpunished.

The onus for justice lies with Rwanda, Africa and the international community to make certain that the will and the resources are available. Then comes reconciliation. To seek to short-circuit this process is to risk seeing history repeat itself.

# 7. If Anyone Is Listening, Where Is the Hope?

Church people in my experience usually want to know where to find hope when they hear about a situation as tragic as that of Rwanda.. The question can be an irritating one if it implies a quest for cheap grace, so that those listening to a litany of woe need not think about the causes and the background and the venality of people and systems. Perhaps it is the only way our frail human spirit can survive such outbursts of violence and bloodshed — unless of course we simply turn away because Rwanda is too far away or too culturally different or too intractable or too lost in the welter of tragedies that have turned our post-cold war world into the nightmare it has become for many people.

## The church of the future

Of course, there has to be hope or our God-given humanity would not survive. In Rwanda the hope lies in the courage of that small band of people who understood their Christianity in non-ethnic terms, who walked justly and mercifully and courageously and paid a shocking price in physical and material terms for their faithfulness. They are the church which Jesse Mugambi says cannot die, the Surviving Church. There *is* hope, and there are clear signs that out of their sacrifice will rise again an institution tempered by its ordeal, committed to the gospel of justice, peace and reconciliation and ready to work for the kingdom. That is one hope.

Another hope is the tremendous resilience of the African spirit, with its ability to look despair in the eye, to laugh, to point to the wide, unending horizon where the big red sun sinks so fast it is gone before you know it and to say there is something better coming tomorrow when it rises. It is a spiritual thing, this hope, which is worn like a skin and covers the whole of life.

There must also be hope that the goodwill of millions of people who tried to help will surmount the failure of leaders and communities to act in a moral and ethical way, so that those humanitarian instincts, uninformed and misguided as some of them were, will not be lost in our disgust at our own unwillingness to do what is right rather than what is expedient. This hope is that we will learn something from this genocide, something our parents and grandparents said we had learned after the second world war.

Rwanda is already old news, and that is our first mistake. Just because a disaster fades from our television screens does not mean it is resolved or that the worst is not yet to come. All the expertise, all the years of experience, all the warnings, all the signs, all the mammoth resources at the disposal of the international community could not stop the genocide or alleviate the suffering. We could not read or did not act upon the signs of the times. Indeed, as the more thoughtful of the aid agencies are now saying, we accomplished almost the opposite of what we intended; and if we do not learn from that, the future, not just for Rwanda or Africa, is extremely unhopeful.

Long before President Juvenal Habyarimana was shot out of the sky, monitors and peacekeepers were in Rwanda from Africa and overseas watching the implementation of the Arusha Accords. The churches were part of that process and worked until the last, dreadful hours signalling that events were not as they should have been. Warnings of an impending disaster, although few knew exactly how bad it might be, went out, but no one listened to the calls for reconciliation.

After April 6, a genocide was unleashed. The UN passed resolutions, evacuated foreigners, pulled out its peace-keepers, vainly tried for a ceasefire, debated the genocide, sent its troops back, set up a tribunal. Still a million people died, and millions more are homeless. The UN relief agencies and international NGOs raised hundreds of millions of dollars, fed and cared for millions of refugees, bought thousands of four-wheel drive vehicles, deployed hundreds of professional emergencies officers who used all the vast experience they had gained in some of the worst hell-holes in the world over the last four decades. It was a masterpiece of logistics and a human tragedy. It was like the old saying: the operation was a success but unfortunately the patient died. Still, no one listened.

The churches in Rwanda and their partners outside knew that something dreadful was being planned, a final solution, and some raised lonely voices of protest and warning. They became fixated on projects of conflict resolution and peace and reconciliation, diplomacy and humanitarian relief. They formed a consortium to work more effectively and to raise funds more efficiently. They responded to outcries of horror and demands to do something — and it was good. It was ecumenism at its best, but the churches of Rwanda are split not so much denomination-ally as ethnically. And no one is listening.

In Africa, the churches and the OAU watched in horror and spoke early and strongly, condemning the genocide and urging support for the accords they had worked so hard to achieve. But it was too late, and they had no resources; and there was too much going on in South Africa and Malawi, in Mozambique and Angola, in Sudan and Somalia, in Liberia and Nigeria. No one listened to marginalized Africa.

So if everyone did so many things right and did them the way they were supposed to, what went wrong? Why were so many people massacred? Why were there so many refugees and displaced people? Why did so many die of cholera? Why?

More questions than answers, but these and other questions need discussion and soul-searching; and there is not much time for that in a world which has changed more in the five years since the cold war ended than in the previous 40 years — and nowhere more than in Africa. The world is a very dangerous place, so we have to try to get it right. And the old ways and the old expertise probably will not work.

I am haunted when José Chipenda says he is not interested in the future of the church, but in the Church of the Future. It is a great slogan, but what does it mean? Actually, it seems to me it is quite biblical. It has to do with Jesus' warning against putting new wine into old wineskins. It means that all the old certainties, like the cold war, are no more, and we have chaos and anarchy to contend with rather than capitalism and communism. Our tried and true methods of coping do not work. What Chipenda is talking about has more to do with a faithful search for new ways, new structures, new concepts and new theologies than mere reforms that will help the church survive for a few more years. Perhaps it is also a return to fundamentals like justice, peace and reconciliation rather than the soothing feelings which so often drive humanitarianism.

Whatever else it means, in Africa it will mean an African church — culturally, spiritually, morally, physically. That will be difficult for Africa and for its partners, but then the future has always been difficult.

## A call to self-examination

The debate on what went so terribly wrong in Rwanda centres on these same things. Much of the self-examination being undertaken by relief agencies has to do with standard operating procedures which did not work right and may fail again in other emergencies. Assumptions by the international community, in the face of Habyarimana's endless delays and prevarications, that diplomacy and conflict-resolution and human rights were what Rwanda really wanted were simply wrong. What the extremists who were in control really wanted was a final solution to the Tutsi problem, a fascist solution really, one which we may see more of as the chaos following the death of communism sets in.

But our humanitarianism could not wrap its thinking around genocide, so we did what we have always done and tried to help the victims rather than stop the victimization. When the blue berets left because their mandate was so vague they could not even defend themselves, let alone others, it was open season for the killers. The same thing happened when the floodgates burst into Tanzania and Zaire. The international agencies moved fast and fairly efficiently, as one would expect of experts and professionals. This was their speciality — no room for enthusiastic amateurs here. The only problem was that the killers fled along with the refugees and, as it turns out, were in control of them. So our humanitarianism fed both without distinction and allowed for reorganization and retaining and re-equipping the old army to take up its final solution again, or at least to try. For some agencies that posed a serious moral and ethical dilemma. How do you deal with a genocide in a humanitarian way? There are no rules in the rule book.

These are questions to be dealt with by the boards, commissions and committees of agencies, including CWA-R and its successors. The debate is already raging, making the fund-raisers very nervous. It was not supposed to be this way. What happens now, though, in the near future in the grim situation of the camps and the country? The UN has decided, using the old rules, not to send a peace-keeping force into the camps to separate the refugees from their masters, so it seems unlikely that many will return to Rwanda. The Hutu army seems bent on restarting the war in one way or another. The RPF is equally committed to doing whatever it feels is necessary to prevent that from happening.

While aid money continues to pour into the camps, now basically controlled by the extremists who we believed had lost the war, the government is flat broke with very little hope that it can improve the conditions of its internally displaced people, let alone manage the return of a million or more refugees. While expatriate aid workers use satellites to fax their reports to Geneva or London or New York or Toronto, the government cannot pay its civil servants. Is something wrong here?

CARE is one of the world's most experienced emergency agencies. Its Canadian executive director John Watson raised many of these issues in a probing analysis published in the *Toronto Globe and Mail* just before Christmas 1994:

> As the Rwanda tragedy unfolds, the entire apparatus of humanitarian intervention in places like Rwanda, Somalia and Bosnia requires a radical re-think. On every level of management old habits, procedures and attitudes must give way. There will be more Rwandas and Bosnias. The changes are not insurmountable. They require the international community to develop new and creative ways of dealing with the unique post-cold war contexts where there is no functioning state. They also require that we begin to recognize and deal with the reappearance of an old enemy — fascism — that is rearing its ugly head in new and virulent forms.

* * *

If the international community can move into that debate honestly and expeditiously, and if the Church of the Future can move beyond mere survival to its basic mission of preaching justice, peace and reconciliation — that is hope. I hope someone is listening.

# Appendix 1
# War Correspondents: A Byline Written in Deep Despair

Journalists are thought to be a callous lot, and much of the time we are. But my experience with colleagues who have seen much of the cruelty of the world is that they take suffering very hard. Like cops, they usually see people — aggressors and victims — at their worst. They also see them over and over again.

Most journalists react to atrocities in three stages. In the first stage when they are very young (or very inexperienced), they respond with shock and revulsion and, perhaps, a twinge of guilty excitement that they are observing something others will never observe: life at its dreadful extremes.

In the second stage, the atrocities become familiar and repetitive, and journalists begin to sound like Spiro Agnew; if you have seen one loss of dignity and spirit, or one loss of limb or loss of a head, you've seen them all. Too many journalists get stuck at this stage. They get bogged down in the routineness of the suffering. Embittered, spiteful and inadequate to their work, they curse out their bosses at home for not according them respect; they hate the people on whom they report.

Worst of all, they don't allow themselves to enter the third stage, in which everything gets sadder and wiser, worse and strangely better.

This is the stage that sets in after years of observing the varieties of destruction of which people are capable. For one thing, you realize the destruction will never stop. People will always find a way to kill one another, inflicting as much pain and torment as possible. If you take away their H-bombs, they will draw their machetes.

What's more, they require very little in the way of an excuse or outside encouragement. Take Rwanda. Say that the pitiless slaughter of the Tutsis is entirely tribally motivated or that it is entirely politically motivated. But then you see a five-year-old boy with his arms cut off, and you know that under all the other rational inspirations lies one that is purely, savagely human.

In the third stage, something happens to one's own work. In stage one, you persuade yourself that the mere telling of the war story is valuable because the people who read it will know what they did not know, and some may act on that knowledge. In stage two you don't care about any of that and, anyway, you don't believe it.

In stage three you continue not to believe it, and you have years of proof to support your hopelessness. Words do not lead to deeds, not good ones. If something improves a bit in one place, it disintegrates in a dozen others.

Sitting around a table telling our war stories, as we all do, is somehow mysteriously redeeming. This is all one has, after the years: these war stories. Nothing productive comes of them, no moral lesson emerges and yet they make impressions so painful that people are compelled to tell them, and others are compelled to listen.

*Roger Rosenblatt*

*US journalist Roger Rosenblatt wrote this from Nairobi, Kenya, for* The New Republic. *It was reprinted in the* Toronto Globe and Mail, *June 11, 1994, and is used here by permission of* The New Republic.

# The "Hutu Ten Commandments"

1. Every Muhutu should know that a Mututsi woman, wherever she is, works for the interest of her Tutsi ethnic group. As a result, we shall consider a traitor any Muhutu who:
— marries a Tutsi woman;
— befriends a Tutsi woman;
— employs a Tutsi woman as a secretary or a concubine.

2. Every Muhutu should know that our Hutu daughters are more suitable and conscientious in their role as woman, wife and mother of the family. Are they not beautiful, good secretaries and more honest?

3. Bahutu women, be vigilant and try to bring your husbands, brothers and sons back to reason.

4. Every Muhutu should know that every Mututsi is dishonest in business. His only aim is the supremacy of his ethnic group. As a result, any Muhutu who does the following is a traitor:
— makes a partnership with Batutsi in business;
— invests his money or the government's money in a Tutsi enterprise;
— lends or borrows money from a Mututsi;
— gives favours to Batutsi in business (obtaining import licences, bank loans, construction sites, public markets).

5. All strategic positions, political, administrative, economic, military and security should be entrusted to Bahutu.

6. The education sector (school pupils, students, teachers) must be majority Hutu.

7. The Rwandese armed forces should be exclusively Hutu. The experience of the October war has taught us a lesson. No member of the military shall marry a Tutsi.

8. The Bahutu should stop having mercy on the Batutsi.

9. The Bahutu, wherever they are, must have unity and solidarity, and be concerned about the fate of their Hutu brothers:
— the Bahutu inside and outside Rwanda must constantly look for friends and allies for the Hutu cause, starting with their Bantu brothers;

— they must constantly counteract the Tutsi propaganda;
— the Bahutu must be firm and vigilant against their common Tutsi enemy.

10. The Social Revolution of 1959, the Referendum of 1961 and the Hutu Ideology must be taught to every Muhutu at every level. Every Hutu must spread this ideology widely. Any Muhutu who persecutes his brother Muhutu for having read, spread and taught this ideology is a traitor.

*December 10, 1990*